W9-AWU-969

CHER

WOMEN of ACHIEVEMENT

CHER

Connie Berman

CHELSEA HOUSE PUBLISHERS
PHILADELPHIA

Frontispiece: Cher arrives at the premiere of *If These Walls Could Talk,* a 1996 HBO film she codirected and costarred in. Often considered outrageous and controversial, Cher has nonetheless risen to the top of the entertainment world.

PRODUCED BY 21st Century Publishing and Communications, Inc., New York, N.Y.

Chelsea House Publishers
EDITOR IN CHIEF Sally Cheney
ASSOCIATE EDITOR IN CHIEF Kim Shinners
PRODUCTION MANAGER Pamela Loos
ART DIRECTOR Sara Davis
DIRECTOR OF PHOTOGRAPHY Judy L. Hasday
COVER DESIGNER Takashi Takahashi

© 2001 by Chelsea House Publishers, a subsidiary of Haights Cross Communications. All rights reserved. Printed and bound in the United States of America.

The Chelsea House World Wide Web address is
http://www.chelseahouse.com

First Printing
1 3 5 7 9 8 6 4 2

Library of Congress Cataloging-in-Publication Data applied for.

ISBN 0-7910-5907-3 (hc) ISBN 0-7910-5908-1 (pbk)

CONTENTS

WOMEN of ACHIEVEMENT

Jane Addams
SOCIAL WORKER

Madeleine Albright
STATESWOMAN

Marian Anderson
SINGER

Susan B. Anthony
WOMAN SUFFRAGIST

Clara Barton
AMERICAN RED CROSS FOUNDER

Margaret Bourke-White
PHOTOGRAPHER

Rachel Carson
BIOLOGIST AND AUTHOR

Cher
SINGER AND ACTRESS

Hillary Rodham Clinton
FIRST LADY AND ATTORNEY

Katie Couric
JOURNALIST

Diana, Princess of Wales
HUMANITARIAN

Emily Dickinson
POET

Elizabeth Dole
POLITICIAN

Amelia Earhart
AVIATOR

Gloria Estefan
SINGER

Jodie Foster
ACTRESS AND DIRECTOR

Betty Friedan
FEMINIST

Althea Gibson
TENNIS CHAMPION

Ruth Bader Ginsburg
SUPREME COURT JUSTICE

Helen Hayes
ACTRESS

Katharine Hepburn
ACTRESS

Mahalia Jackson
GOSPEL SINGER

Helen Keller
HUMANITARIAN

**Ann Landers/
Abigail Van Buren**
COLUMNISTS

Barbara McClintock
BIOLOGIST

Margaret Mead
ANTHROPOLOGIST

Edna St. Vincent Millay
POET

Julia Morgan
ARCHITECT

Toni Morrison
AUTHOR

Grandma Moses
PAINTER

Lucretia Mott
WOMAN SUFFRAGIST

Sandra Day O'Connor
SUPREME COURT JUSTICE

Rosie O'Donnell
ENTERTAINER AND COMEDIAN

Georgia O'Keeffe
PAINTER

Eleanor Roosevelt
DIPLOMAT AND HUMANITARIAN

Wilma Rudolph
CHAMPION ATHLETE

Elizabeth Cady Stanton
WOMAN SUFFRAGIST

Harriet Beecher Stowe
AUTHOR AND ABOLITIONIST

Barbra Streisand
ENTERTAINER

Elizabeth Taylor
ACTRESS AND ACTIVIST

Mother Teresa
HUMANITARIAN AND
RELIGIOUS LEADER

Barbara Walters
JOURNALIST

Edith Wharton
AUTHOR

Phillis Wheatley
POET

Oprah Winfrey
ENTERTAINER

Babe Didrikson Zaharias
CHAMPION ATHLETE

"REMEMBER THE LADIES"

MATINA S. HORNER

"Remember the Ladies." That is what Abigail Adams wrote to her husband John, then a delegate to the Continental Congress, as the Founding Fathers met in Philadelphia to form a new nation in March of 1776. "Be more generous and favorable to them than your ancestors. Do not put such unlimited power in the hands of the Husbands. If particular care and attention is not paid to the Ladies," Abigail Adams warned, "we are determined to foment a Rebellion, and will not hold ourselves bound by any Laws in which we have no voice, or Representation."

The words of Abigail Adams, one of the earliest American advocates of women's rights, were prophetic. Because when we have not "remembered the ladies," they have, by their words and deeds, reminded us so forcefully of the omission that we cannot fail to remember them. For the history of American women is as interesting and varied as the history of our nation as a whole. American women have played an integral part in founding, settling, and building our country. Some we remember as remarkable women who—against great odds—achieved distinction in the public arena: Anne Hutchinson, who in the 17th century became a charismatic

7

religious leader; Phillis Wheatley, an 18th-century black slave who became a poet; Susan B. Anthony, whose name is synonymous with the 19th-century women's rights movement, and who led the struggle to enfranchise women; and in the 20th century, Amelia Earhart, the first woman to cross the Atlantic Ocean by air.

These extraordinary women certainly merit our admiration, but other women, "common women," many of them all but forgotten, should also be recognized for their contributions to American thought and culture. Women have been community builders; they have founded schools and formed voluntary associations to help those in need; they have assumed the major responsibility for rearing children, passing on from one generation to the next the values that keep a culture alive. These and innumerable other contributions, once ignored, are now being recognized by scholars, students, and the public. It is exciting and gratifying that a part of our history that was hardly acknowledged a few generations ago is now being studied and brought to light.

In recent decades, the field of women's history has grown from obscurity to a politically controversial splinter movement to academic respectability, in many cases mainstreamed into such traditional disciplines as history, economics, and psychology. Scholars of women, both female and male, have organized research centers at such prestigious institutions as Wellesley College, Stanford University, and the University of California. Other notable centers for women's studies are the Center for the American Woman and Politics at the Eagleton Institute of Politics at Rutgers University; the Henry A. Murray Research Center for the Study of Lives, at Radcliffe College; and the Women's Research and Education Institute, the research arm of the Congressional Caucus on Women's Issues. Other scholars and public figures have established archives and libraries, such as the Schlesinger Library on the History of Women in America, at Radcliffe College, and the Sophia Smith Collection, at Smith College, to collect and preserve the written and tangible legacies of women.

From the initial donation of the Women's Rights Collection in 1943, the Schlesinger Library grew to encompass vast collections documenting the manifold accomplishments of American women. Simultaneously, the women's movement in general and the academic discipline of women's studies in particular also began with a narrow definition and gradually expanded their mandate. Early causes, such as woman suffrage and social reform, abolition, and organized labor were joined by newer concerns, such as the history of women in business and the professions and in politics and government; the study of the family; and social issues such as health policy and education.

Women, as historian Arthur M. Schlesinger, jr., once pointed out, "have constituted the most spectacular casualty of traditional history. They have made up at least half the human race, but you could never tell that by looking at the books historians write." The new breed of historians is remedying that omission. They have written books about immigrant women and about working-class women who struggled for survival in cities and about black women who met the challenges of life in rural areas. They are telling the stories of women who, despite the barriers of tradition and economics, became lawyers and doctors and public figures.

The women's studies movement has also led scholars to question traditional interpretations of their respective disciplines. For example, the study of war has traditionally been an exercise in military and political analysis, an examination of strategies planned and executed by men. But scholars of women's history have pointed out that wars have also been periods of tremendous change and even opportunity for women, because the very absence of men on the home front enabled them to expand their educational, economic, and professional activities and to assume leadership in their homes.

The early scholars of women's history showed a unique brand of courage in choosing to investigate new subjects and take new approaches to old ones. Often, like their subjects, they endured criticism and even ostracism by their academic colleagues. But their efforts have unquestionably been worthwhile, because with the publication of each new study and book another piece of the historical patchwork is sewn into place, revealing an increasingly comprehensive picture of the role of women in our rich and varied history.

Such books on groups of women are essential, but books that focus on the lives of individuals are equally indispensable. Biographies can be inspirational, offering their readers the example of people with vision who have looked outside themselves for their goals and have often struggled against great obstacles to achieve them. Marian Anderson, for instance, had to overcome racial bigotry in order to perfect her art and perform as a concert singer. Isadora Duncan defied the rules of classical dance to find true artistic freedom. Jane Addams had to break down society's notions of the proper role for women in order to create new social situations, notably the settlement house. All of these women had to come to terms both with themselves and with the world in which they lived. Only then could they move ahead as pioneers in their chosen callings.

Biography can inspire not only by adulation but also by realism. It helps us to see not only the qualities in others that we hope to emulate, but also, perhaps, the weaknesses that made them "human." By helping us identify with the subject on a more personal level they help us feel that we, too, can achieve such goals. We read about Eleanor Roosevelt, for instance, who occupied a unique and seemingly enviable position as the wife of the president. Yet we can sympathize with her inner dilemma; an inherently shy woman, she had to force herself to live a most public life in order to use her position to benefit others. We may not be able to imagine ourselves having the immense poetic talent of Emily Dickinson, but from her story we can understand the challenges faced by a creative woman who was expected to fulfill many family responsibilities. And though few of us will ever reach the level of athletic accomplishment displayed by Wilma Rudolph or Babe Zaharias, we can still appreciate their spirit, their overwhelming will to excel.

A biography is a multifaceted lens. It is first of all a magnification, the intimate examination of one particular life. But at the same time, it is a wide-angle lens, informing us about the world in which the subject lived. We come away from reading about one life knowing more about the social, political, and economic fabric of the time. It is for this reason, perhaps, that the great New England essayist Ralph Waldo Emerson wrote in 1841, "There is properly no history: only biography." And it is also why biography, and particularly women's biography, will continue to fascinate writers and readers alike.

Waving to the audience, Cher holds her 1999 World Music Awards trophy for her lifelong contribution to the music industry. This award, produced by Marcor International, honors the world's best-selling recording artists of the past year. Cher has continued to delight audiences with her music and stage performances for decades.

1

AND THE BEAT GOES ON

In 1998, at the age of 52, singer, actress, entertainer Cher recorded "Believe," the song that became the biggest hit of her career. It sold more than 11 million copies worldwide and for weeks reigned at number one on the charts in the United States and Great Britain. *Billboard* named "Believe" number one on its Hot 100 Singles list for 1999, and the song earned Cher a Grammy Award.

Probably one of the most significant triumphs for Cher, however, was how the song changed the life of a sick little boy named Eric Campbell. Eric was only 11 years old, but he was suffering from a life-threatening brain tumor, and the doctors thought that surgery was too risky. Several times every week, Eric endured radiation treatments, which the doctors hoped would shrink the tumor.

Each time Eric journeyed to and from the hospital, he listened to his special song, "Believe," sung by Cher, one of his favorite singers. Whenever he heard the song, Eric urged his mom to turn up the volume on the radio. The song made it a lot easier for Eric to bear his hardship.

The story doesn't end there, however. Cher learned about Eric through a remarkable organization called the Make-A-Wish Foundation. Touched by his plight, she decided to surprise the boy with a visit. Although in the midst of a cross-country concert tour, Cher detoured to Tampa, Florida, to see Eric, who was probably one of her most devoted fans. He certainly qualified as one of her youngest.

Cher arrived looking every inch the star. Striding into Eric's room in spiky high heels and gem-studded jeans, she gave the astonished little boy a giant hug and a big kiss. When Eric told her how much her singing inspired him, she replied that his courage inspired *her* as well. Then she hugged him again. Eric gave Cher a tiny rose pin and a thank-you card decorated with a butterfly.

After the meeting, Eric said he was amazed that a superstar like Cher actually made a special trip to meet him. "She told me I was good," Eric remembered. Anytime Eric thinks it all may have been a dream, he gazes at the snapshot of them together. "I like her music," Eric enthuses. "I think it's good, and well, I think she's pretty, even though she's older than my mom and dad. And gosh, my dad is like 30."

At an age when many performers are either retired or contemplating retirement, Cher is still a preeminent figure in the entertainment world. For more than four decades, she has been delighting audiences, often shocking and provoking but never boring them. Her first hit on the music charts was "Baby Don't Go," a duet with partner Sonny Bono. Thirty-four years later, Cher was on the charts again with "Believe."

Early in 1999 Cher aired her television special, *Cher: Live in Concert from the MGM Grand in Las Vegas,* a show nominated for an Emmy Award. Proving that she could still strut her stuff, she emerged from the floor of the stage outfitted in boots with a long velvet cloak and wearing a long red wig. For nearly an hour, her energetic performance electrified the audience. Along with seemingly endless costume changes, all of which displayed her incredibly toned and muscled body, Cher delivered some of her biggest hits, including "Believe."

Some 37 years before, Cher was just a naive teenager when she teamed up with Sonny Bono, a guy sporting a Prince Valiant hairdo. With partner Sonny, she first made her mark as the female half of the unforgettable act Sonny and Cher. The duo's popularity as singing hippies soared and then faded when their brand of folk rock was replaced by hard rock. Not ready to call it quits, Sonny and Cher revised their act, making it more glamorous and sophisticated, and staged a short-lived comeback.

When the couple's act finally broke up, in real life as well as on television, many believed Cher could never make it on her own. But she proved them wrong. A determined Cher emerged as one of the most popular concert and night-club entertainers in show business. In her later acting career, she garnered several Academy Award nominations and even a Best Actress Oscar. Another successful solo comeback in the 1990s is a tribute to Cher's enduring appeal. Hit singles, film roles, and stellar performances have repeatedly put her back on top.

Cher's life has been one of drama and inspiration as she rose from an often impoverished and disrupted childhood to stardom. No film Cher might ever star in could possibly be as fascinating as her own life story, which began more than 50 years ago in the little California town of El Centro, near the Mexican border.

Cher performs in Toronto, Canada, during the 1999 tour to promote her album Believe.

Nine-year-old Cher poses as if already a star. Growing up, she often faced periods of poverty and instability in her home but dreamed of a better future and of the day she would be famous.

2

HUMBLE BEGINNINGS

Cherilyn Sarkisian was born on May 20, 1946, in El Centro, California, the daughter of Jackie Jean Crouch and John Sarkisian. The little girl, who would later be known simply as Cher, inherited her dark hair and striking looks from her mother, who is part Cherokee Indian, and her Armenian father. John Sarkisian was handsome, charming, and suave. He was also a gambler and a drug addict. Jackie Jean, who later changed her name to Georgia Holt, had show business ambitions and sometimes worked as a model and bit-part actress.

Cherilyn's parents carried on a stormy relationship. Years later, a grown Cher told an interviewer, "I think I was about ten months old when she [Georgia] left my father for the first time and went to Reno for a divorce." The Reno divorce was only the first one. Georgia and John were married and divorced two more times.

After the first divorce from John, Georgia married another man. Cher doesn't even remember the man's name because she was so young. The third of Georgia's eight marriages was to an actor, John Southall, the father of Cher's half-sister, Georgeanne. Although Georgia's marriage to Southall lasted only five years, Cher has said that she considers John Southall her real father. She remembers him as a good-natured man who turned belligerent when he drank too much. John and Georgia often fought violently and separated several times. Finally, when Cher was nine years old, they split permanently.

Georgia's many marriages and subsequent divorces created a nomadic existence for Cher and Georgeanne. They were constantly on the move and usually had little money. Cher remembers using rubber bands at one time to hold her shoes together. At one point, Georgia was forced to put Cher in an orphanage. Though Georgia visited Cher every day, it was a painful time for both mother and daughter. Georgeanne later said, "Mom remembers it as the most traumatic thing in her life."

Still, there were some good times when Georgia had work. Cher remembers going to Ensenada, Mexico, with her mother and some friends. They stayed in cheap hotels and had fun on the beach.

Cher also recalls getting into trouble because of her sister. Once Cher was baby-sitting and gave her sister a toy car to play with. Little Georgeanne promptly swallowed the rubber wheels. Her mother was hysterical, and Cher got sent to her room, wondering what she had done wrong.

Cher revealed her feisty personality as early as the fourth grade. On "sharing day," when all of the kids were going to tell what they had done last summer, Cher rebelled. She thought the idea was stupid, and she said so. "I'm going home," she declared, and got up and walked out of school. When she told her mother and grandmother, who was living with the family at the time, what had happened, they laughed, obviously admiring Cher's independent nature.

The family members probably also took notice of

Cher's creativity at a young age. At the end of fifth grade, Cher put on a show for her teacher and her class. She "produced" the musical *Oklahoma!* Cher got a group of girls together and directed and created the dance routines. Since she couldn't get the boys to take part, Cher acted the men's roles and sang their songs. Even at that age, she had an unusually low voice. There were no costumes and not a lot of time to rehearse, but the class still applauded and cheered for the performers. It was Cher's first taste of pleasing her public.

A park in El Centro, California, where Cher was born. The small town is located about 85 miles east of San Diego, near the border to Mexico.

Cher and her mother, Georgia, share a get-together in 1987. Cher's relationship with Georgia, who was herself an aspiring actress, has not always been happy, but Cher has said that her mother is still a very special person in her life.

Despite the often hard times and the instability of her mother's marriages, Cher had one persistent childhood ambition: to be famous. She spent endless hours signing her name again and again, perfecting her autograph. She fantasized about her future, standing in front of a mirror and pretending to be a celebrity. Young Cher carried on imaginary conversations with reporters, admonishing them to leave her alone.

Although she felt she was unattractive and not very talented, she stayed true to her dream. As she later commented to an interviewer, "I couldn't think of anything that I could do. . . . I didn't think I'd be a singer or dancer. I just thought, well, I'll be famous. That was my goal."

As Cher grew into her teens, still dreaming of being somebody, circumstances changed. In 1961, Georgia married a bank manager, Gilbert La Piere. He adopted both Cher and Georgeanne and enrolled them in a fancy private school, Montclair Prep, in the well-to-do community of Encino, California. Students at the school wore gold charm bracelets and cashmere sweaters; many had their own personal telephones at home. Like Cher's stepfather, the fathers of Montclair Prep students held high-paid jobs and were financially successful.

Such posh surroundings presented a challenge for Cher, and the teenager stood out from the others in both her striking appearance and outgoing personality. A former classmate, Barbara Dulien, recalled, "I'll never forget seeing Cher for the first time. She was so special. I even remember what she wore, a tweed suit, a tank sweater and her hair up on her head in a tight little bun. She was like a movie star, right then and there." Dulien added, "We all came from wealthy families. But to us, Cher was a star already. She said she was going to be a movie star and we knew she would."

Cher was not a movie star yet, but she behaved like

one when she entertained other students during lunch hour. Flinging back her long, coal-black hair, she belted out songs in her throaty contralto voice. She no doubt shocked a few when she displayed flashes of the daring fashions for which she would one day be famous. Cher was the first young woman in her crowd to wear a midriff-baring top.

In classes, Cher was not a top student. She did well in French and English, however, and she was intelligent and creative. She usually got good grades on term papers and essays. Later, as an adult, Cher would discover that she had suffered from a learning disability called dyslexia, a condition that limits a person's ability to read.

Cher's conduct at school was another matter. "I've always had a very childish rebellious streak," Cher has said of herself. Her nonconformist behavior often sent her to the principal's office for breaking some school rule. When she appeared with oversize sunglasses and a black, broad-brimmed hat and was told to remove them, she defiantly refused. She was imitating film star Audrey Hepburn and dressing as Hepburn did in the 1961 film *Breakfast at Tiffany's.*

It appeared that Cher, who was fascinated by movie stars, had taken on Audrey Hepburn as a role model. Cher remembers being disappointed that there were no dark-haired actresses she could copy or even aspire to be like. She has said, "All I saw was Doris Day and Sandra Dee. . . . In the Walt Disney cartoons, all the witches and evil queens were really dark. There was nobody I could look at and think, 'That's who I'm like.'"

Then Cher saw *Breakfast at Tiffany's,* in which Hepburn portrayed Holly Golightly, an eccentric, fast-living young woman in New York City. Here was a dark-haired, captivating star with whom Cher could identify, and she began to pattern her outfits and behavior after the character portrayed by Hepburn.

Audrey Hepburn, as she appeared in the 1961 film Breakfast at Tiffany's, *was Cher's role model. The young girl imitated the actress by wearing sunglasses and a hat similar to those worn by Hepburn.*

Still, Cher was an insecure teenager. Because of her exotic appearance, which would later fascinate audiences, she felt different and alone. She desperately wanted to fit in, to "belong," to be like the popular girls at Montclair with their perky flip hairdos. When she expressed her disappointment to her mother, Georgia reassured her daughter that one day she would be glad to "stand out."

For Cher, at 16, it did not seem like going to school was the way to become famous. So, she dropped out, left her mother's house, and moved in with a girlfriend in Los Angeles. Cher took some acting lessons and bounced around from job to job to support herself. Sometimes she danced in small clubs along Hollywood's famed Sunset Strip. While most of the town was fast asleep, young Cher was dancing her heart out in the wee hours of the morning. Ever hopeful, despite the odds of making it in show business, she made the rounds, introducing herself to performers,

Sunset Strip in Los Angeles was the scene of Cher's early attempts to break into show business. After leaving home at age 16, she began her career dancing in the clubs along the famed "Strip."

managers, and agents. The teen did not hesitate to approach anyone she thought could help her get a break, make a new contact, or get an audition.

Then, in November 1962, at a coffee shop on Hollywood Boulevard, Cher met the man who would change her life. His name was Salvatore Philip Bono, known as "Sonny." At 27, Sonny did not have a sparkling career as an entertainer. He was a junior assistant to record producer Phil Spector, the genius behind the special sounds of such popular '60s groups as the Ronettes and The Righteous Brothers.

When they first met, Cher was not overwhelmed by

Sonny. Years later she recalled: "I didn't even like him that much. I just thought, 'That is the weirdest-looking man I've ever seen.' I mean, he was ugly."

Sonny was certainly not a young woman's dream. He was short, had a long nose, spoke in a whiny voice, and wore an odd haircut. But he was in show business, and like Cher, he was eager to be a star. Something clicked between the two, and from that modest meeting in a coffee shop, important events soon unfolded.

A chance meeting with Sonny Bono helped launch the young 16-year-old woman on the road to stardom. Sonny was as determined as Cher to be successful, and their partnership as recording artists and television and nightclub entertainers delighted audiences for a decade.

3

SONNY AND THE ROAD TO STARDOM

Sixteen-year-old Cher was skinny and gawky and something of an oddball. But Sonny felt that this teenager was capable of great things, and he later found out she also could sing. "In the first two weeks I knew her I told her that she could be a great star. That's what she wanted," Sonny later recalled.

Although at first Cher wasn't attracted to Sonny, she did find something special about him. "He looked like Julius Caesar," she remembers. "But it was like one of those bolt-out-of-the-blue moments when something inside you just says, 'From this second, you're never going to be the same again.'"

Shortly after meeting Sonny, Cher's girlfriend moved out of their apartment, and Cher was on her own. With little money and few prospects, she took up Sonny's offer to move in with him. It was purely friendship, Sonny said. He would pay the rent, and she would clean and cook. Sonny, however, got the worst of the bargain. Cher didn't like cooking and cleaning. She often stayed out all night and slept most of the day. A writer once noted that it was a good thing Cher had a voice, or Sonny might have thrown her out on the street.

Cher and Sonny's relationship was bound to change. Cher has admitted that after a few months, she developed a major crush on her roommate. Sonny, she thought, was a worldly man who knew about the music business. He was good to Cher, looking after her and allowing her to trail after him to recording studios, where she could meet and mingle with singers and musicians. It was a thrill for Cher. She has said that back in 1963, she was a rapt and eager student, always listening, watching how Sonny dealt with stuff. "I took every opinion he had and made it my own," Cher recalled.

Like Cher, Sonny had great ambitions to be "somebody," hopefully in the world of rock music. He played drums and sang backup for various groups. One day in 1964, when Sonny was on the drums at Phil Spector's recording studio, there was a sudden need for a backup singer. Turning to Cher, who was waiting for Sonny, Spector ordered her to "get out there" and start singing.

Cher had gotten her lucky break. Soon, she was working regularly as a backup singer and collecting a regular paycheck. While not a featured singer, she did backup on some of Phil Spector's rock and roll classics, including "You've Lost That Lovin' Feeling" and "Be My Baby." She even recorded her own single, "Ringo, I Love You." More importantly, however, Cher was becoming more than just Sonny Bono's friend. She was becoming a performer in her own right.

Late in 1964 Cher and Sonny became romantic partners. Recognizing that they were really in love, the couple performed their own wedding ceremony in a hotel room in Tijuana, Mexico, exchanging rings and vowing eternal love. Although they told people they were married, the ceremony was hardly official.

At the same time, Cher and Sonny launched their professional partnership. Their first gigs were as a duo

Cher and Sonny proudly display their first gold record. Written by Sonny, the song "I Got You, Babe" was a tremendous hit in 1965.

called Caesar and Cleo. Sonny had the idea that they could cash in on the publicity from the on-screen, off-screen romance of Elizabeth Taylor and Richard Burton, who had starred in the epic film *Cleopatra*. The name didn't work. Their first record, "The Letter," bombed, as did another, "Love Is Strange."

Still the couple persisted, and in 1965 Cher and Sonny had a hit. Written by Sonny, the song "I Got You, Babe" was certified gold when it sold its first one million copies, and it went on to sell more than three million copies. The story of a young couple who are poor but have each other is an enduring folk-rock song.

Other hit singles followed, including "The Beat Goes On" and "Bang, Bang," the latter of which was Cher's first solo recording. She and Sonny were climbing toward the top as recording artists. With further tunes on the charts, including "Baby, Baby," "What Now My Love," and "All I Really Want To Do," it seemed as though the whole country was listening to—and talking about—Sonny and Cher. Before she was 20, Cher had realized her goal of becoming famous.

However, Cher was not in charge. Sonny was the boss, and Cher was happy to let him take the lead. As she later said, "I was delighted for [Sonny] to take care of everything. I thought he was the tower, the pillar of strength and maturity and intelligence."

Having gone back to their original names, Sonny and Cher, the singing duo appeared in concerts and on television. Adopting a hippie style, they attracted a wealth of publicity—and fans. Sonny clowned on stage in kooky "mod" outfits: bell-bottom pants, Eskimo boots, and a wild shirt, all covered with a long fur vest and often topped by a knit cap. Cher imitated Sonny's outfits and added heavy makeup. Comedians at the time joked that it was hard to tell which was Sonny and which was Cher.

Even when the couple wasn't performing, they clung to their outrageous outfits. Hollywood's fanciest restaurants (which the famous couple could easily afford) did not always welcome Sonny in his boots and long vest or Cher with her ostrich-skin slacks and polka-dot fur jacket. "We were always getting kicked out of places because of how we dressed," Cher remembers.

Such escapades only made them more popular, as did their onstage antics. They were playful and affectionate with each other. Sonny called Cher "squaw" and Cher retaliated by calling him "a short Italian." They seemed to spend more time clowning and showing off their costumes than singing.

Sonny and Cher were not actually living a hippie lifestyle. That was just their act. Sonny was simply too old to be a youthful rebel, and he didn't really want to be. And Cher did not share the hippie philosophy of "dropping out" of the mainstream. She wanted to be part of the material world. Also, the couple made no secret of their antidrug views. As one observer noted, they may have looked onstage as if they were under the influence of drugs, but they definitely were not.

As the 1960s came to a close, Sonny and Cher's popularity began slipping, and they weren't topping the charts anymore. Hard rock was taking over the music scene. The heavy, loud sound of groups like Jefferson Airplane and Cream made the folk-rock music of Sonny and Cher seem too bland. In an attempt to recapture their young audience, the dynamic duo produced a film called *Good Times*. Released in 1967, the film featured the couple in various silly skits. In one skit they sang and romped around in jungle costumes portraying Tarzan and Jane; in another they donned raincoats and slouch hats and acted out the roles of a couple of private detectives.

Good Times did not appeal to the couple's fans, and it was a flop. Disappointed but undeterred, Sonny and Cher shot another film, *Chastity*, released in 1969. Written and directed by Sonny, who did not appear in the film, it told the story of a young woman, Cher, searching for the meaning of life. Although *Chastity* was also a monumental flop, some critics were taken with Cher's performance. *Cue* magazine wrote, "Cher has a marvelous quality that often makes you forget the lines you are hearing."

Along with the release of *Chastity*, Sonny and Cher celebrated two important events. When Cher discovered she was pregnant, she and Sonny were legally married in early 1969. A few months later, the couple welcomed a little daughter. They named her Chastity, after their second film.

The film Good Times *featured Cher and Sonny in skits that were supposed to display their comic talents. Fans were not amused by scenes such as this jungle sketch, and the film flopped.*

The joys of parenthood, however, did not solve the couple's problems. After two box-office bombs and a decreasing audience for their records, Sonny and Cher were almost broke. They had spent some $500,000 and mortgaged their home to make *Chastity*. It was time for a change.

In 1970 Sonny and Cher discarded the love beads, funky clothes, and outlandish hairdos. Turning to the nightclub circuit, they appeared as a new, sophisticated, and mature act. Sonny sported designer tuxedos, and Cher adopted glamorous, often low-cut gowns that would become her signature outfits. The couple really hit the big time when they played

Las Vegas, Nevada, with their new look.

Once again Sonny and Cher were in the spotlight. Wooed by television executives the couple began landing guest appearances on prime-time shows. After a particularly impressive gig on *The Merv Griffin Show* in 1971, CBS programming director Fred Silverman offered the duo their own variety show—*The Sonny and Cher Comedy Hour.*

Debuting on August 1, 1971, the show was an instant hit. During its three seasons on the air, it ranked near the top of the ratings. Once again, fans applauded the couple's comedy, as Cher with a deadpan expression gently ribbed Sonny about his looks

The top-rated Sonny and Cher Comedy Hour *offered songs, cheerful banter, and comic routines. In this parody of* The Wizard of Oz, *Sonny appears as the cowardly lion and Cher as Dorothy.*

and short stature. Sonny and Cher exuded an aura of warmth, playfulness, and caring that only enhanced their appeal. Viewers were further enchanted when little Chastity also appeared on the show. They seemed like a perfect family.

The couple's offstage life, however, was anything but perfect. As the show went into its second season, viewers were unaware of what was happening behind the scenes. Sonny and Cher's onstage banter belied the ill will and resentment the couple harbored for each other. Joking on the show turned to mutual strife as soon as filming stopped.

As time went on, Sonny and Cher had more nasty spats, fighting over even the smallest of issues. Their quarrels were sometimes aired in public. During one rehearsal for a nightclub act in 1972, they argued so heatedly that Cher stormed offstage in a huff. The engagement was abruptly canceled, the excuse being that Cher was ill. Thus began a pattern of canceled performances, supposedly because Cher was sick. The unspoken truth was that the two were fighting and didn't want to appear together.

Part of the problem, according to one observer at the time, was that "[t]hey live together 24 hours a day, seven days a week—and not many married couples do that." With their marriage all but over, each began seeing other people. As Cher recounted to *Rolling Stone*, "I remember singing 'I Got You Babe' and then thinking I can't wait to get to the beach to see my boyfriend."

Gossip columnists and reporters speculated about the trouble between the couple, including the "boyfriend" Cher had met in 1973, David Geffen. A record-company executive, Geffen offered to help untangle Cher's financial problems and guide her career. For two years Cher and Geffen had a romantic relationship, which was no secret, especially to Sonny, who was furious.

For months, stories abounded in the media. Then, in February 1974, Sonny filed for a separation, citing "irreconcilable differences." A week later, Cher countered with a divorce suit. She charged Sonny with "involuntary servitude," claiming that he withheld money from her and deprived her of her rightful share of their earnings. Many of the couple's court battles revolved around finances.

The divorce proceedings dragged on for months, with charges and countercharges and a custody battle over Chastity, who in the end lived with her mother. While the divorce battle rolled on, Sonny and Cher each tried to find success in solo television shows. Sonny's program, *The Sonny Comedy Review*, debuted in fall 1974 and was canceled in the middle of the season.

Cher's show, simply called *Cher*, was produced by Geffen. Centered on Cher's songs, monologues, and comedy performance, the show proved successful at first. But it later ran into censorship problems—partly because of Cher's revealing outfits—and began slipping in the ratings. Cher later explained what happened: "I dreaded doing the monologues, because I was so bad at them, and I got tired of fighting the censors and the producer."

Despite the bitterness of their divorce, which became final in June 1975, Cher still missed Sonny. She reached out to him, asking if he would like to team up again in a new show. A surprised Sonny agreed, and the new *Sonny and Cher Show* debuted as a summer replacement in 1976. It was lambasted by the critics. "Sonny and Cher are back together, and the excitement is underwhelming," wrote *Variety*.

The show was canceled after only one season. As a duo in show business, Sonny and Cher were finished. Over the years, Cher's feelings about the man who had been such a large part of her life, emotionally and professionally, remained in conflict.

In public, Cher often made nasty comments to the press, belittling Sonny. Then in another moment, she would express fondness for him, as she did even during their divorce proceedings. "I wanted to be mad at him," she said. "I *was* mad at him. But I couldn't stay mad at him; there was this stupid thing between us that I couldn't cut, something in that strange, gray Sonny and Cher zone." Cher has explained that the bond between them was like a spiritual connection in which each knew that if the worst happened, one would be there for the other.

After the divorce and two failed television shows, Cher's career was on shaky ground. Some observers thought she could not make it without Sonny's guidance. Others doubted the extent of her talent. Cher, however, was determined to succeed. She mustered the same strong will and ambition that had thrust her into the limelight in the first place and focused on succeeding as a solo performer. The world of entertainment was about to discover just how much Cher could accomplish on her own.

Despite their breakup and often bitter recriminations, Cher still performed professionally with Sonny from time to time. Here the two belt out a song at a 1979 taping of the Mike Douglas Show.

Cher projected a new glamorous and sophisticated image as she struck out on her own. Finally free from Sonny's control, she was determined to reach her goal of stardom as a recording artist.

4

GOING SOLO

During the early 1970s, while still with Sonny, Cher had released a number of singles, including her tremendous hit "Gypsies, Tramps, & Thieves." The wild number showcased her sexy contralto voice, and the single hit the top of the charts almost immediately. The albums *Cher* and *Foxy Lady* that followed soon after proved modestly successful. Next came *Bittersweet White Light*, an album that Sonny had produced, which was a complete disaster.

In the mid-1970s, Cher cut more albums and singles, and received mixed reviews. A critic for *Rolling Stone* thought that the songs "Dark Lady" and "Train of Thought" from her 1974 album *Dark Lady* were "catchy tunes," and that "Cher's voice is so attractive, one senses possible future directions."

For Cher, "future directions" meant trying to realize her dream of becoming a hard-rock singer. With the help of David Geffen, she signed with Warner Brothers Records and produced *Stars* in 1976, at the same time she was doing her solo television show. Geffen encouraged Cher to perform the kind of songs in the album that she didn't normally sing. *Stars* included tunes made famous by musicians such as Eric Clapton and Neil Young, and even a 1950s bebop ditty from the Everly Brothers.

Cher and the producers had high hopes for *Stars*. Although Cher has claimed she doesn't care what critics think, she must have been disappointed with the reviews. One critic wrote that in singing the songs of other artists, she came off sounding "secondhand." Another was even more blunt. "Cher," the reviewer wrote, "is just no rock and roller. . . . Image, not music, is Cher Bono's main ingredient for both records and TV."

Image was indeed a major part of Cher's popularity during the 1970s. She was glamorous, daring, and out-spoken, and the media loved her. She earned hundreds of thousands of dollars in her nightclub acts, singing and showing off lavish and often outrageous costumes, includ-ing some that were nearly transparent. She appeared regularly on television as a provocative guest who entertained viewers with her witty one-liners and daring outfits. Cher's cherished ambition to be "somebody" had propelled her, and her alone, into the limelight.

Gossip columnists also encouraged Cher's flamboy-ant image by continually writing about her various romantic involvements, and Cher was never shy about revealing such information to interviewers. She was very candid, for instance, about her affair with David Geffen when they became a hot item. When Geffen gave her a diamond ring, Cher gushed to an interviewer: "I asked David to buy it for me because I wanted to feel that someone loved me enough to give me something I could wear." She went on to confess: "I'm very much in love with David Geffen. At first I was upset about my split from Sonny, but thanks to Dave's love and devotion, Sonny's just an old memory."

The romance with Geffen was brief, however, as Cher grew restless with his control over her life. Willing at first to accept Geffen's guidance, especially concerning her divorce proceedings, Cher came to resent his advice on every little matter. She was enjoying her freedom from Sonny, who had run her life for so many years, and she wanted to be her own woman. To Cher, Geffen was trying to take over where Sonny had left off. Although they remained friends, with Geffen encouraging her singing and advising her about her nightclub act, by 1975, even before the divorce from Sonny was final, the romance with Geffen was over.

Years later, David Geffen commented that Cher "was the woman I loved most of all." Cher later shared her feelings with a reporter as well, saying, "We were really crazy about each other." Madly in love or not, Cher bounced back rather quickly when she fell in love again. Her next choice was rock musician Gregg Allman, whom she had first met in 1974 at a nightclub in Hollywood.

Gregg Allman sang with the Allman Brothers band, which had enjoyed a successful run with its rock music. When Gregg spotted Cher in the audience that night, he wrote her an admiring note and asked her for a date. Cher was immediately attracted to the young man with the long, blond hair and the hip good looks. She talked to him backstage, and they made a date for later that same night.

Still involved in the divorce tangle with Sonny, Cher was seen everywhere with Gregg, and the gossip columnists had a field day with their relationship. More frenzy followed when only a few days after her divorce from Sonny, Cher married Allman in a ceremony in Las Vegas, Nevada. Nine days later, she left him. "Gregg and I have made a mistake," she explained, "and I have always believed it best to admit one's mistakes as quickly as possible."

The split was only temporary and for the next two years—from 1975 to 1977—Cher and Gregg carried on a stormy relationship, separating and reuniting several times. People often wonder why Gregg was so appealing to Cher. He was a very troubled person—an alcoholic who used cocaine and was addicted to heroin. Cher knew of his addictions, but she claimed later that she was naive and unaware of the terrible hold that drugs could have on users. In her memoir, *The First Time*, Cher admits that staying with Allman "was the wrong thing to do, but there was something about Gregory. He was handsome and wild. He was rock 'n' roll—the definitive Bad Boy; he was also tender and sensitive."

Another reason for Gregg's appeal was that Cher believed he would not dominate her, as Sonny and David Geffen had. She thought Allman was not the kind of man who would "box" her in because, as she put it, "it wasn't in him to put that box together."

Gregg may not have tried to control Cher, but he was the ultimate male chauvinist. His idea of a wife was one who made the beds, cooked the meals, and cleaned the house. Cher was a lot of things, but she certainly was not a housekeeper. Gregg became very jealous of Cher's professional relationship with Sonny during their short-lived television reunion in 1976. Gregg wanted Cher with him more of the time, since his band had broken up by then, and he had nothing to do. Cher was constantly worried that he was drinking or on drugs. And Gregg couldn't stick to his promises; Cher often came home to find him using drugs with his junkie friends.

However, Cher wanted the relationship to work, especially when she learned she was pregnant. The prospect of a baby drew the couple together. Their son, Elijah Blue, was born in July 1976, and it appeared that their marriage was going to work after all. Gregg went into rehabilitation, and he seemed to have overcome his problems with addiction.

In 1977, with a one-year-old son and Gregg back on track, Gregg and Cher cut an album together. Titled *Two the Hard Way,* it seemed to epitomize the couple's on-again, off-again relationship. There was also debate on how they would be billed on the album. Neither liked "Gregg and Cher," so they decided on calling themselves "Allman and Woman."

Cher and her second husband, rocker Gregg Allman, share a happy moment as the proud parents of a baby son, Elijah Blue. Cher's stormy relationship with Allman ended a year later.

The album featured some rock songs by Cher, which were not well received by critics or fans. According to one biographer, the public wanted Cher to sing pop, not rock. The cover also stirred controversy, with Gregg and Cher appearing half-naked in a tangled embrace.

To promote the album, Cher and Gregg went on tour, which soon resulted in a disaster. Gregg began drinking heavily, and Cher finally realized that he had returned to his previous behavior. Although she was a resilient woman and did love Gregg, she couldn't endure the bad times anymore. Years later, recalling her painful decision, Cher explained, "I realized it was never going to be any different. . . . And I finally became bored. That sounds capricious of me or whatever, but I knew I was the one who was trying to put the strength into him."

Cher's marriage was over, and it seemed as if her recording career was slipping away too. For her next album, *Cherished*, the producers at Warner Brothers insisted she return to her pop style. Still determined to be a rock singer, Cher hated working on the songs. One engineer in the recording studio commented, "You could tell that she would really have rather been doing just about anything [rather] than recording those particular songs." The pop album fizzled and the record company dropped Cher.

A single mother with two children, Cher realized that she had to make a choice about the direction of her singing career. Deciding to temporarily abandon her desire to be a rocker, she accepted the offer of Neil Bogart of Casablanca Records to cut a disco music album. In the late 1970s, disco music, with its loud, rhythmic, danceable beat, was becoming very popular. But Cher hated disco, believing that it was superficial and could hardly be considered serious music. Despite her lack of enthusiasm, she did cut a single, "Take Me Home," about a woman asking a man in a singles bar to take her home.

The single and the album *Take Me Home* became instant hits and remained bestsellers for more than half of 1979. With such success, Cher seemed to change her mind about disco, declaring "I never thought I would want to do disco . . . [but] it's terrific! It's great music to dance to. I think that danceable music is what everybody wants."

Perhaps adding to the album's popularity was its memorable cover. Cher appeared decked out as Brunhilde, the legendary woman warrior of ancient German myths. Complete with a horned helmet and metal breastplate, Cher's outfit ranks as one of her most eye-catching.

Encouraged by the popularity of *Take Me Home*, Cher planned to return to rock music. She may have said she now liked disco, but she still wanted to sing rock. In her next album, *Prisoner*, the producer wanted to take advantage of Cher's image and the media obsession with her. The resulting memorable cover shows her as a "prisoner" of the press, draped in chains.

Unfortunately, *Prisoner*, also released in 1979, didn't work. Much of the fault lay with Cher herself. She insisted on including some rock songs rather than

In 1980 in New York City's Central Park, Cher performed with boyfriend Les Dudek as lead singer of the band Black Rose. The band folded soon afterward, as did Cher's romance with Dudek.

Although Cher's solo career as a rock artist was faltering, she still packed the audiences in at her nightclub shows in Las Vegas. These glitzy and glamorous performances kept her in the public eye and on top as a performer.

going all disco. That and her uneven singing style made the album unfocused, with no clear musical direction.

In 1980, still determined to realize her dream of becoming the queen of rock, Cher began a relationship with rock musician Les Dudek, and the two formed a group called Black Rose. Although Cher was the lead singer, she did not receive top billing. Presumably she wanted to create the impression that all band members were equal.

That was difficult to do. Even with a drastic change in her hairstyle, Cher was easily recognized when she stood in front of the band and sang. She had cut her hair to nearly a buzz cut and dyed it bright yellow, green, and pink, trying for a "punk" look. Black Rose appeared on television, but the band failed to land concert dates. The group's album, *Black Rose*, was also a total failure.

Before long, Black Rose broke up. Although Cher vowed that she and Les would remain a couple anyway, each soon began dating other people and the romance petered out.

Even with a faltering recording career, Cher still packed listeners in at her Las Vegas nightclub performances. She dazzled audiences with her glamour and her glitzy shows, and she was earning as much as $300,000 a week. Cher may not have been recognized as a top rocker, but she was well known as a famous singer and television and nightclub personality.

Apparently, just being famous was not enough for Cher. Although people told her she was at the pinnacle of her career, she remained unsatisfied. Her next step would be revealed when film director Francis Ford Coppola met her backstage after one of her shows. "You're so good," he said. "Why aren't you doing movies?"

In 1981 the bright lights of Broadway beckoned Cher to New York City, where she began an acting career that would carry her to the heights of fame.

5

OSCAR-WINNING ACTRESS

Cher had always wanted to act in films, but the powerful producers and directors in Hollywood did not take her seriously as an actor. By the early 1980s she had no films to her credit except the amateurish *Good Times* and *Chastity*. Coppola may have thought she was good, but no other filmmakers seemed to.

Then, while doing a television special with Shelley Winters, the famous actress gave Cher some good advice. Shelley told Cher that if she was really serious about acting, she should go to New York City. "Don't . . . talk about it—just do it," said Shelley.

In 1981, with her children in tow, Cher moved to New York City, hoping to begin her acting career on Broadway. She enrolled Chastity in the prestigious High School of Performing Arts and began trying to get auditions herself. Cher was thrilled to be in the Big Apple. She has claimed that she never liked Los Angeles, saying the city is like a drug that eventually kills the people living there. In L.A., she claimed, "Nobody wants to say anything good about you."

Cher firmly believed that New York would be more open-minded about her determination to act. She also loved the hectic pace of the city. She enthused to gossip columnist Cindy Adams, "New York's the hippest of all. Here everything's different. I walked out in a beaded wig, a blanket around me, no make-up, and construction workers hollered, 'Heeeyyyyy Cheeerrrrr!' They ran up for autographs. L.A. doesn't do that."

Although she was dating Gene Simmons, star of the rock band Kiss, Cher was not under a man's control for the first time in years. She attended parties by herself, met new people, and made new friends. As she said, "I've met the best people since I've been here. This is the first time in my life that I ever had a friend."

Thanks to her mother, who knew the wife of esteemed director Robert Altman, Cher got a lucky break. Altman had directed such successful films as *Nashville* and *M*A*S*H*. Georgia told Cher that Altman was casting a Broadway play called *Come Back to the Five and Dime, Jimmy Dean, Jimmy Dean*. Cher expressed interest in playing a role in the play, and Georgia passed the message along to Altman's wife.

Robert Altman was a savvy businessman as well as a gifted director. He knew that the play, which was written by an unknown midwestern playwright named Edward Graczyk, would have added appeal with a celebrity like Cher in it. Cher soon began rehearsing the part of Sissy, the voluptuous waitress who works as a counter girl in the dime store where the play is set.

Come Back to the Five and Dime, Jimmy Dean, Jimmy Dean tells the story of the reunion of six members of a James Dean fan club in a small Texas town. Twenty years earlier, the women had thrilled to the presence of Dean in their own small town, where he was filming the movie *Giant*. Then tragedy struck early one morning in September 1955, when Dean died in a car crash. The play is one of remembrance and revelation, as the six women talk about what had happened then and in the ensuing years.

In her first theater performance, Cher shared the stage with a roster of fine actresses, including Kathy Bates, Karen Black, Sandy Dennis, Marta Heflin, and Sudi Bond. However, the play received mediocre reviews, although some critics liked Cher's work. In *The Village Voice,* critic Andrew Sarris wrote that Cher was "the revelation of the play." Another reviewer praised Cher as "assured and vigorous. She also does quite well in her character's demanding second-act soliloquy that takes her from anger to tears to raucous laughter."

During the play's run, Cher made friends with Sandy Dennis, and the two often huddled together, talking and giggling. Another costar, Karen Black, was not so accepting. Black had never become a major film star, but she had done excellent work in films such as *Easy Rider.* She did not give Cher much support onstage.

The other cast members were friendly enough with Cher. Although she was doing good work in her first stage

Cher's rise as a talented actress began with her performance in the Broadway play Come Back to the Five and Dime, Jimmy Dean, Jimmy Dean. *She received critical praise for her portrayal of a member of a James Dean fan club that is holding a 20-year reunion. The film was Cher's first since* Chastity, *in 1969.*

role, they were not so thrilled with the fans that Cher drew to the performances. Kathy Bates once complained, "It's her fans. They bring flash bulb cameras to the show—every night. That just isn't done in Broadway houses."

Although the play had only a brief run, Altman directed a screen version as well. The movie, which cost about $800,000 (which for most films is a very small budget), was shot in 17 days and starred the same cast. In contrast to the play, the film received some favorable reviews. Altman was praised for his direction, and the cast for its portrayals. Cher was singled out by critic Pauline Kael in the *New Yorker* magazine. "Cher is simple and direct in her effect," Kael wrote, "as if it were the easiest thing in the world to slip into the character of an aging small-town belle with a Texas accent."

Before the film came out, Cher received another movie offer. Following a Wednesday matinee of the stage show, someone knocked on her dressing-room door. Film director Mike Nichols had seen the show, and he was intrigued with Cher's performance. He offered her a role in a film he was directing about the life and death of Karen Silkwood.

In the 1970s, Karen Silkwood had worked in a plutonium-processing plant in Oklahoma. When she discovered that the plant was violating important safety regulations, exposing her and the other workers to deadly radiation, she decided to report the offense, offering documents and papers as evidence. On her way to meet a news reporter, Silkwood was killed when her car ran off the road. The documents she was carrying were never found. Many believed the crash was no accident and that Silkwood had been murdered to destroy her incriminating testimony.

According to Cher, when Nichols asked her if she wanted a role opposite celebrated actress Meryl Streep, who would play the main character, Karen Silkwood, Cher accepted the offer without even asking what the film was about. A couple of weeks later, Nichols told Cher

that she would be playing Dolly Pelliker, a rebellious, tough-talking lesbian who shares a house with Karen and Karen's boyfriend, Drew, played by Kurt Russell.

Cher was thrilled at the opportunity to work with Mike Nichols and Meryl Streep. When she thought more about the film and who she would be working with, however, Cher had an attack of nerves. "I thought there was no actress working who compared with Meryl," she later wrote. "She was simply better than anybody else—and how could I possibly share the same screen with her?"

Cher should not have been apprehensive. Meryl Streep too was a bit worried about appearing with Cher, confessing that "I felt intimidated at the very thought of meeting Cher. I mean, in photos she always looks so wonderfully thin, and so beautiful and stylish. The first thing that struck me when we did meet was

As a boisterous but vulnerable gay woman in the film Silkwood, *Cher won acclaim and an Academy Award nomination for her performance. Meryl Streep (left), appeared in the leading role of Karen Silkwood.*

how different she is in private life from the public image of her. Cher seemed, well, like anyone else. Very real. Very honest."

Cher's role as Dolly was not very glamorous. She wore no makeup, and her hair was not styled. Her usual costume was an old bowling shirt and a pair of chino pants. Once Cher tried a simple touch—curling her eyelashes. Mike Nichols put a stop to that right away: Cher was going to play a woman who was not preoccupied with her physical appearance.

Working on *Silkwood* was one of Cher's most enjoyable film stints. She and Streep became good friends, and the more experienced actress gave Cher some helpful advice. Meryl Streep told Cher that she had fine acting instincts and counseled her against taking acting lessons. Streep felt that instruction would stifle what she believed was Cher's considerable natural ability.

For Cher, being with the cast was like being with a family. Besides her friendship with Meryl, Cher felt very close to Kurt Russell. Kurt clowned on the set with Cher, stealing bites of her food and throwing her funny looks during filming. She thought of Kurt as a "bossy big brother," and she loved his carefree antics.

When *Silkwood* opened in 1983, audiences were skeptical about Cher's ability as an actress. She has often repeated the story about the audience's reception at a preview that Cher attended. At the beginning of the film, when her name flashed across the screen in the credits, the audience laughed. Cher was devastated. Her sister, who was with her, began to cry. Cher didn't cry, but she was deeply hurt.

The preview audience changed its attitude by the end of the film. Hollywood also took notice at last, and so did the critics. "Kurt Russell and Cher . . . [give] performances to match Meryl Streep's," wrote one reviewer. Cher received her first Academy Award nomination, for Best Supporting Actress, and won a Golden Globe Award. Although Cher lost out on the Oscar to Linda

Hunt for her role in *The Year of Living Dangerously*, she had achieved an incredible triumph by garnering such recognition for her first major film.

Following the enthusiastic response to *Silkwood*, Cher was deluged with film offers. She turned them down until she found one she really wanted. She chose another film based on a true story. *Mask* is the story of Rusty Dennis, played by Cher, a single mother who hangs out with bikers in a motorcycle gang. The young actor Eric Stoltz portrayed Rusty's teenage son, Rocky, who suffers from craniodiaphyseal dysplasia, a disfiguring condition that enlarges the head and distorts the facial features.

Rusty, although rebellious and sometimes a drug user, loves Rocky unconditionally. She assures him that his internal beauty is far more important than what people see at first glance. Rocky's disease not only disfigures him but also makes his internal organs weak. Rocky Dennis dies while still a teenager. One of the film's most haunting scenes is Rusty's discovery one morning that her son has died in his sleep. She cradles Rocky in her arms before she says good-bye.

Cher enjoyed working with Eric Stoltz, but she was often at odds with the director, Peter Bogdanovich. In 1966, Bogdanovich had written an unflattering article about Cher and Sonny. Cher noted in her memoirs that she thought the incident was past and gone, but the director, she thought, still harbored ill feelings toward her. She believed that he didn't like her because she was too "edgy," as she put it. According to Cher, the director didn't even like bikers, who are a large part of the film.

To understand her role, Cher became friends with Rusty Dennis, whom she regarded as an inspiration and a true heroine. If Cher thought some of her lines did not agree with Rusty's character, she told Bogdanovich. She sometimes refused to play a scene the way Bogdanovich directed it because she thought it was wrong.

Bogdanovich was a well-known director with some

In a scene from the film Mask, *Cher, as the real-life Rusty Dennis, visits the cemetery to ponder her son's untimely death. Cher turned in an exceptional performance that won her a Best Actress Award at the Cannes Film Festival in 1985.*

clout in the film business. By defying him, Cher was taking a chance. She recalled in an interview that he threatened to replace her. "Don't forget, I can cut around you and leave you out. It's about the boy," he said. Today Cher says, "I never listened to [Bogdanovich's] direction because I never liked it. I didn't feel he knew what Rusty was about as well as I did."

Cher survived the ordeal by following Eric Stoltz's advice. He suggested that she do what he did: "When he [Bogdanovich] tells you something, you just go 'Yes, yes, yes,' and then you do it your way, and he never notices. Watch me." Cher saw that what Eric said was true. She recalls, "And I thought, okay, I could do that. I started saying 'Yes, yes, yes,' and Peter never noticed."

In 1985, for her role in *Mask*, Cher walked off with Best Actress Award at the Cannes Film Festival in France.

It seemed that ignoring Bogdanovich had been a good idea. Both Cher and Stoltz received rave reviews, but the film faded away. Cher thought the studio did not publicize it enough, claiming the promoters wouldn't put her picture in ads and on posters.

Cher was even more distressed when she was not nominated for an Academy Award for Best Actress. She had expected to receive this recognition, and others had told her she should be nominated. "I was really upset," she remembered. "I wanted to throw up and die." Part of the reason for her not being nominated could have been because *Mask* did not do well at the box office. It may also have been, as Cher herself noted, that Hollywood was once more snubbing her.

However, the Academy Award officials did ask her to attend the awards ceremony that year and present an Oscar. Cher accepted and presented the Best Supporting Actor Award to veteran actor Don Ameche for his role in *Cocoon*. At the ceremony Cher showed Hollywood that she was not a person to be ignored. She turned up in one of the most outrageous costumes she had ever worn. She had told her designer, Bob Mackie, that she wanted to look like a Mohawk Indian. Mackie came up with an incredibly bizarre outfit that included a see-through breastplate of black diamonds and beads. Cher draped a black cashmere blanket decorated with Indian symbols over her shoulder and wore tight pants covered by a long skirt. And to top it all off, she wore a Mohawk headdress.

People certainly paid attention. One observer said Cher's headpiece seemed suitable for the funeral of Darth Vader. Another quipped that she looked like a float at Mardi Gras.

As a result of her role in *Mask*, Cher became involved with a charity that continues to be one of her favorites. The National Craniofacial Foundation helps children with disfiguring diseases such as the one that took the life of Rocky Dennis. Cher is not

Backstage at the 1985 Academy Awards, Cher poses with actor Don Ameche, to whom she had presented an award for Best Supporting Actor in the film Cocoon. *Her fantasy costume prompted critical quips, which Cher ignored.*

just a figurehead lending her name. She has served as honorary chairwoman from time to time, helped with publicity, and attended fund-raising functions.

In the late 1980s, Hollywood was no longer ignoring Cher. She was featured in three major motion pictures— *The Witches of Eastwick, Suspect,* and *Moonstruck.*

In *Witches,* Cher shared the screen with three accomplished actors—Susan Sarandon, Michelle Pfeiffer, and Jack Nicholson. The story is about three women living in a small New England town with no available men around until a mysterious but charming stranger shows up. Played by Nicholson, the character reveals himself to be the devil. As the story unfolds, the three women turn out to be witches. The film was part fantasy, part supernatural, and part horror.

Cher has complained that *The Witches of Eastwick* director, George Miller, didn't work with the characters and that he had opposed casting her in the first place. According to Cher, Miller didn't want her to "ruin" his movie. There were compensations, however. Jack Nicholson made Cher and her costars feel welcome, and Cher appreciated Nicholson's attention. Cher also become good friends with Michelle Pfeiffer, describing Pfeiffer as "the only friend I trust not to distort or misuse what I say."

Witches was greeted with mixed reviews, but it was a box-office success. The same was not quite true of Cher's next film, *Suspect*. Cher played an overworked lawyer who defends a mute and homeless Vietnam veteran, played by Liam Neeson, who has been charged with murdering a government official. One of the trial's jurors, in a role played by Dennis Quaid, helps Cher discover that the defendant is being framed. *Suspect* received poor reviews as some critics thought the plot had too many twists and that the ending was not very believable. Critics called the film dour and humorless and noted that the glamorous Cher seemed out of place in a plain and not especially appealing role. One reviewer commented, "Cher is trapped trying to play the one thing she's not—dull. . . . It's a dogged, joyless performance."

Cher came into her own, however, and flourished as an actress in her next film, *Moonstruck*. In the movie, Cher played the dowdy, forlorn widow, Loretta Castorini, who works as a bookkeeper in a funeral home and lives with her parents.

Moonstruck is a romantic comedy about a middle-aged Italian widow who sees her life as dull and without passion. Loretta agrees to marry the well-meaning but ordinary Johnny Cammareri, played by Danny Aiello.

While Johnny is gone on a trip, Loretta meets his younger brother, Ronny, played by Nicholas Cage. Ronny is a baker with one hand. At first, there is tension between Loretta and Ronny. Suddenly the sparks fly, and the two soon fall madly in love. Loretta's family is shocked. She is supposed to marry a stable, down-to-earth man. Ronny is eccentric and sometimes even a little unbalanced. The film's title refers to the mysterious charm of the full moon, which shines in the sky during many scenes in the movie. It symbolizes the sudden love that can come out of nowhere and unite two people.

Playwright John Patrick Shanley had written *Moonstruck* as a vehicle for Sally Field. When Field couldn't take the part of Loretta, the producers thought of Cher. Cher really liked the script, but hesitated at first. She thought the story was a bit weird, that the public wouldn't like it, and if the film flopped it might hurt her career.

After several visits from the producer, Patrick Palmer, Cher agreed to do the film. She decided to take a chance. To play the role of Ronny, Cher wanted Nicholas Cage, who had impressed her with his performance opposite Kathleen Turner in *Peggy Sue Got Married*. She said of Cage's talent, "Nicky never plays it safe. You could play a role five different ways, and he'll go to the one where you've got the most to lose."

The producer didn't want Cage at first, and Cher had to fight to get him. Once Cage was in the role and filming began, however, Cher was somewhat put off by Cage's attitude. She found him distant and moody. "He works alone," Cher remarked, "he *acts* alone, and you kind of act alone with him." Cher was not used to such a cool costar.

Moonstruck was directed by Norman Jewison, a well-respected filmmaker. He and Cher got along fine after Cher told him she could sometimes be difficult. Jewison allowed her to improvise and to act in her direct and natural manner.

Well on her way to film stardom, Cher shared the screen with three of Hollywood's major actors in the 1987 film The Witches of Eastwick. *Jack Nicholson looms over his costars (from left to right) Cher, Susan Sarandon, and Michelle Pfeiffer.*

Cher went all out for her role. To get the right accent for an Italian-American woman from Brooklyn, she hired actress Julie Bovasso to coach her. Bovasso also played Loretta's aunt in the film. Cher got further help from her new boyfriend, Rob Camilletti, who had grown up in an Italian-American family near Brooklyn. He gave her advice on the kinds of gestures, the laughs, and all the commotion that often goes on in a large Italian family.

Cher's diligence and determination paid off. Accompanied by a cast that included such prestigious actors as Olympia Dukakis (Loretta's mother) and Vincent Gardenia (Loretta's father), as well as Danny

Cher won a coveted Academy Award for Best Actress in Moonstruck, *in which she transforms herself from a dowdy widow to a glamorous, romantic figure. In this scene from the film she talks with Vincent Gardenia, who plays her father.*

Aiello, Cher was captivating. The touching, humorous Cinderella story earned praise from critics and audiences alike. It was also a commercial hit.

Although the story of a lonely widow who finds love sounds like a soap opera and is rather old-fashioned, it is surprisingly a charming tale with an excellent script. Most critics singled Cher out for her performance. One wrote, "Her capacity as an actress to grow and change with the parts she plays is astounding." The same reviewer was also impressed with her beauty as she transformed herself from sad widow to glamorous woman on her first date with Ronny.

Cher must have been especially pleased when Pauline Kael of the *New Yorker* magazine praised her performance. Kael had blasted Cher for her role in *Suspect.* In her review of *Moonstruck,* the critic described Cher as "devastatingly funny and sinuous and beautiful."

It seemed inevitable that Cher would be nominated

for an Academy Award as Best Actress, and she was. But she had some stiff competition. Old friend Meryl Streep was up for *Ironweed*, Glenn Close for *Fatal Attraction*, Holly Hunter for *Broadcast News*, and Sally Kirkland for *Anna*. Cher did not expect to win over such veteran actresses. Later, during an interview, Cher recalled her feelings on the night of the Academy Awards:

> The night I won the Oscar, it was bizarre because I was sitting there and when Paul Newman started reciting the nominees, I just started going deaf, I mean really deaf. And then when he opened the envelope and he looked down at the paper, he took a breath and I thought, "Well, I didn't win, because you don't need a breath to say Cher. I thought "That's it." Only he said "Cher." I guess he needed a breath to say "Cher." And then all I knew was that Robert Camilletti was there and Chastity was there and they stood up and I didn't realize that the rest of the place stood up, I didn't realize anything.

At the 1988 Academy Awards ceremony Cher did not appear as the dowdy widow she had portrayed. She stepped onto the stage in a typical Cher costume: a black pajamalike creation of flowing gauzy fabric that revealed her well-muscled body. Although the costume was provocative, Cher looked truly lovely, almost petite and delicate despite her tall frame. That night, Cher looked like a true movie queen.

While no one disputed that Cher deserved to win, some commentators felt that her Oscar triumph signaled an important change in Hollywood. Not only did Cher appear in a negligeelike outfit, but she also danced onstage—and was applauded for her daring. As Douglas Brode wrote in his book *The Films of the Eighties*: "In the early eighties, her [Cher's] personal style and off-camera antics may have been too much to accept, despite the star's box office allure and the quality of her work. But by decade's end, the old guard had passed and the hip new Hollywood perceived in Cher—see-through, bare-nearly-all outfits, frizzed

An exultant Cher hugs her Oscar, just presented to her by actor Paul Newman at the 1988 Academy Awards. In capturing the award, Cher had finally triumphed after years of snubs from Hollywood.

hair, frankly stated and unbleeped opinions—a person quite appropriate to them."

Hollywood had finally accepted Cher as one of them.

Cher has more than once declared that winning her Oscar is one of the most meaningful moments of her life, comparing it to her joy at the birth of her children. She also claims that she never thought about winning an Oscar while filming *Moonstruck*. Cher says that Meryl Streep once told her to never take a part to win an Academy Award. "It's just a great bonus," said Streep. But Cher admits that she had wished for an Oscar.

Does Cher's Oscar occupy a special place in her home? In 1999, she told *People* magazine that she uses it as a doorstop for her bedroom door. "My cats have to run in and out and it's the perfect weight," she said. "Some people think it's disrespectful but I don't think of it that way."

In a mere six years, Cher had risen from a novice actress in a failed Broadway play to one of Hollywood's most accomplished actresses. She had an Oscar, and she was respected. The world seemed to be at her feet. But as had happened before in Cher's career, just when her star was burning its brightest, it began to flicker. Her next films would jeopardize her reputation as an actress, and she was about to grapple with major disappointments.

Cher, dressed as an Egyptian goddess, promotes her new line of perfume at a 1988 party in New York City. The late 1980s and early 1990s were difficult times for the actress/singer. Cher's film career seemed to be at a standstill, and she had to contend with conflicts in her personal life as well.

6

NOT SUCH GOOD TIMES

During the late 1980s Cher had not given up singing or performing. In 1987 she recorded the album *Cher* and made three videos based on songs from the album. Three albums were to follow: *Heart of Stone* (1988), *Outrageous* (1989), and *Bang, Bang, My Baby Shot Me* (1989). When *Heart of Stone* proved successful, she followed it up with a video of the same title.

It was in her stage shows, however, that Cher found the most financial success. She appeared at Atlantic City, New Jersey, where she received one of the highest ticket prices paid for a show—$200 a seat. She also continued to draw crowds in Las Vegas. In 1989–90 Cher went on tour—*The Cher Extravaganza*—taking her band and backup singers cross-country and into Canada. During these performances Cher sang and showed video clips from her films and her old television shows.

For the most part, critics found her tour enjoyable and liked its nostalgic nature. Some wondered, however, why she indulged in her past by showing what one observer called her video "scrapbook." Others admired her "showmanship" and "star quality." As expected, her fans turned out in droves.

In 1988 Cher decided to introduce her own line of perfume. Called "Uninhibited," a name that seemed quite appropriate for Cher, the line debuted with much fanfare that year. She personally visited department stores to promote the perfume, whose label read "bottled but not contained." Even at the pricey cost of $175 an ounce, Uninhibited sold well. At Macy's department store in New York City, more than 10,000 women showed up for Cher's appearance.

The famous discotheque Studio 54 in New York threw a Halloween party to celebrate Cher and the debut of her perfume. According to observers, the party was a lavish affair attended by celebrities such as actors Sylvester Stallone and Eric Stoltz and feminist author Gloria Steinem. One partygoer commented that Cher dressed with a "combination of gaudiness and taste, as she is now all things to all people."

Uninhibited earned around $15 million in sales in 1988. However, when disagreements erupted over marketing problems, sales dropped off sharply in 1990, the last year the perfume was manufactured.

Despite the huge success of *Moonstruck,* Cher didn't make another film for almost three years. When she finally accepted a role, she played a feisty, kooky divorced mother with two daughters. Released in 1990, *Mermaids* teamed Cher with a young actress named Winona Ryder in the role of the older daughter. In what seemed a replay of her own life, Cher portrayed Mrs. Flax, an eccentric, flamboyant woman always on the lookout for the right man. Since most of her romances are with married men, they inevitably break up, and she and her daughters move on. Despite her unstable lifestyle, Mrs. Flax is a deeply caring mother, and one of the themes of the film is how the bond of love ties the family together.

Cher signed on to the project because she liked the script and because the story reminded her of *Moonstruck.*

FEBRUARY 1988 $1.95

New Woman

How to Know
When He's
the Right Man
and It's the
Right Time to
Fall in Love

10 Keys
to Self-
confidence

STRESS
AND YOUR
STARS
Special Horoscope
to Help You
Lead a
Healthier Life

CHER Delight!
Fully Fledged,
Fantastic,
and 41

Boost Your
Brainpower! 8
Ways to Wise Up

How Good Is Gold?
As an Investment,
That Is!

Is Your Mother
(Perish the Thought)
Envious of You?

Can a Woman Run
the Biggest Media
Empire in the
World? Knockout
New Novel from
Anna Murdoch
FAMILY BUSINESS

Despite setbacks, Cher never stopped being a public person-ality, and people were always curious about her life and romantic attachments. As this 1988 cover of New Woman *magazine proclaimed, Cher's appeal was not entirely waning, and she was still "fantastic" at 41.*

She called it "a sweet look at people who are totally out of their minds and doing the best job they can, but they're just cracked."

The producers believed that Cher would be the star attraction for the film, and they let her have control behind the scenes. However, she often disagreed with director Lasse Halleström about the film's concept. Halleström wanted to add scenes, such as the younger daughter's death, to heighten the drama. Cher insisted that the film be a comedy, like *Moonstruck*. Audiences, she felt, wanted humor, not depressing death scenes. Cher prevailed, and Halleström was fired.

Cher's film family in Mermaids *included English actor Bob Hoskins as her boyfriend and Winona Ryder (left) and Christine Ricci (right) as her daughters.*

Cher also prevailed in getting Winona Ryder to play the role of the older daughter. She had seen the 18-year-old relatively unknown Ryder in the film *Beetlejuice* and liked her performance. Cher invited Ryder to an audition in which the young actress didn't even read any lines. She and Cher simply chatted. The problem was that another young actress, Emily Lloyd, had already been signed for the role. Emily Lloyd later sued the producers when she lost the role to Ryder.

Cher was very much taken with Winona Ryder, and they formed a fast friendship. Cher seemed to feel that she needed to guide the young actress in her career and in her personal life. The two socialized on and off the set, shopping together and going to movies and plays. Cher seemed to be playing Ryder's mother in real life as well as in the film.

Further problems arose when a new director, Frank

Oz, came on board. Oz was best known for directing Muppet movies. Again, Cher objected. The film, she said, was not about puppets but about people. According to Cher, Oz was also making the film too serious. *Mermaids*, she said, should be a "feel-good" film.

Again, Cher prevailed, and Oz left the project. Feelings between Cher and Oz were bitter, and she blamed him for what she considered her poor acting under his direction. Cher felt justified in what she had done, but she was also depressed. "Winona and I cried every night and every day," she recalled. "It was just the worst experience of my life."

The film was way over budget and behind schedule when Richard Benjamin took over as director. A former actor, Benjamin could more easily cajole and even sympathize with temperamental actors. Some incidents arose between Cher and Benjamin when he demanded more from her and called for numerous retakes. Cher did respect Benjamin, however, and the film finally wrapped in December 1989.

Because the studio was unsure about how to advertise the film, producers delayed its release. *Mermaids* finally opened in theaters in December 1990, but it was not a commercial success and the reviews were not spectacular. The *New York Times* wrote that it was "a smooth, unexceptional entertainment about coming of age in a world where truly bad things happen only on television." The *Times* did give Cher a boost, calling her performance "cheeky, broad, comically self-assured." Reviewers liked Winona Ryder as well, and no doubt *Mermaids* helped launch the young actress's future career. Despite the film's subdued reception, today it is considered a cult classic.

Cher has looked back at this time in her career and feels she made critical mistakes: she turned down two leading roles—one in the hit film *Thelma and Louise* and the other in *The War of the Roses*. After the success of *Moonstruck*, she was so worried about her next career move that she was overly cautious.

During the late 1980s, Cher's professional woes were compounded by health troubles, which plagued her physical well-being. Usually energetic and full of pep, she became increasingly exhausted. Even though she carefully watched her diet and didn't smoke or drink, she was terribly rundown. Some days she could hardly drag herself out of bed, and she could no longer put in long days on a movie set or in a recording studio.

Months of tests finally revealed that Cher had "yuppie flu," or by its medical name, chronic fatigue syndrome. Although not life threatening, the disease causes its victims to suffer from debilitating tiredness throughout the day, no matter how much sleep they get.

Cher did not let the condition defeat her. She researched a variety of possible treatments and decided on homeopathy. Homeopathic medicine treats conditions in a nontraditional way, often using vitamins, acupuncture, herbs, and massage. Cher found a doctor who would help her devise a plan of action, including a recommended diet of foods, vitamins, and other supplements.

The treatments took months, but Cher finally began to feel better. She still often felt tired throughout the day, but she found that if she exercised moderately, not her usual four hours a day at the gym, she would gain back some of her energy.

Based upon her own experiences, Cher published an exercise book in 1988. Called *Forever Fit*, the book was written with the help of sports nutritionist Robert Haas. *Forever Fit* reflected Cher's own personal views on exercise and revealed how she worked her way back from her illness to a moderate but still challenging health routine. The book sold about 100,000 copies the year it came out.

While the treatments continued, Cher still had to earn a living to provide for Elijah and Chastity. Clearly, television and film jobs were out; they required long, arduous hours of work. When a friend who made hair products asked Cher to help promote her products, Cher accepted the offer. She needed the money, and she was still too sick to work on other projects.

Cher began making infomercials—television programs, or information commercials, that advertise products. Unlike the usual minute-long television commercials, infomercials can run several hours long while someone talks about the product and demonstrates its uses. Infomercials can publicize anything from exercise equipment to cookware. In Cher's case she promoted health, beauty, and diet products.

Cher has said that her agent advised her not to do infomercials because she would damage her professional reputation. She went ahead anyway, and soon regretted it. She didn't realize that infomercials appeared regularly on many channels. People began making fun of her, just as they had in the days before she had earned respect for her acting. Some accused her of selling out and abandoning her work as an artist. "Suddenly I became the Infomercial Queen and it didn't occur to me that people would focus on that and strip me of all my other things," she told *Ladies Home Journal.*

Cher found herself the butt of various comedians' jokes. Late-night talk show hosts often mocked her as a regular part of their opening monologues. Soon, her physical illness was exacerbated by depression.

The situation reached an unfortunate climax the night that Cher made a disastrous appearance on *The David Letterman Show* in 1993. When Letterman snidely referred to the infomercials, she lost her temper and called him an obscene word. Even though the show is prerecorded and the station bleeped Cher's remark during the broadcast, the audience could still read her lips. While Cher sincerely regrets the incident today, she admits she couldn't deal with it at the time. "He made me squirm and that's how I reacted," she told *Interview* magazine later. News of the confrontation

Cher and daughter, Chastity, share a loving relationship. But it took time for Cher to come to terms with Chastity's announcement that she was gay.

grabbed the headlines, and gossip columnists loved it. Cher's response was to stay away from the talk-show circuit.

During the late 1980s, Cher was forced to confront a host of personal and family issues. Even before she began working on *Mermaids*, she had been stunned when in 1988 Chastity stated openly that she was a lesbian. Angry and upset, Cher reacted without thinking, and screamed at her daughter the next time she saw her. Part of Cher's anger stemmed from the knowledge that everyone but she had known about Chastity, including her father. There was also a touch of guilt in Cher's reaction. She thought she had done something wrong in raising her daughter.

Cher later expressed her feelings about Chastity's orientation in an interview: "We got into a huge fight about it and it took me at least a month to begin to come to terms with it. I felt that I had failed as a parent." She recalled that she was "devastated" and blamed herself for not spending more time with Chastity when she was growing up. When Cher was performing away from home for weeks—or even months—at a time, others took care of her daughter. Cher also thought that Chastity was making a terrible decision and that the media would "crucify" her.

Chastity did not dispute this. In her book *Family Outing,* her account of growing up as the child of Sonny and Cher, she said that she did believe that her mother had left her alone too much. Chastity complained that too often her mother put her career before her children.

Cher does not disagree. She has frankly admitted, "I couldn't argue with it. In one way or another my job's always taken precedence. I gave up spending enough time with my children. You know, there are some things that you do well, and that wasn't one of them for me."

Eventually Cher came to understand her own feelings about her daughter's sexuality. In her memoir, she explained, "I had to realize that Chas had to live her life in the way that made her happy; she was still Chas. . . . She was my child, and it wasn't good enough for me to *just* accept her. I had to support her and be proud of *who she was.*"

Another personal conflict arose between Cher and her son, Elijah Blue, when he decided to quit high school to focus on a career as a rock musician. She wanted him to finish school for what she called "character reasons." Cher may very well have regretted her own failure to complete high school. She was so angry about Elijah's decision that she didn't speak to him for almost three months. Since they lived in the same house, it was an uncomfortable situation.

Mother and son also argued about Elijah's appearance. The young man looks very much like his father, rocker Gregg Allman. And when Elijah shaved off his eyebrows and colored his naturally blond hair black, Cher was furious, telling him she couldn't stand his appearance. "He looks like Moe of the Three Stooges," she told an interviewer.

The disagreement blew over, and Elijah returned to his blond locks. Today, he is one of Cher's most frequent escorts when she attends Hollywood functions. Despite any squabbles she has had with her children, they all share a strong bond, and Cher is proud of them. "They're basically good people," she says. "They're both concerned about people less fortunate than they are."

Perhaps Cher's most wrenching experience during this time was her breakup with Robert Camilletti. Eighteen years younger than Cher, Rob had captured her heart when she met him in 1986 in New York City while filming *The Witches of Eastwick*. Cher has admitted that they didn't have a lot in common: he was not very worldly, did not read much, and didn't share Cher's taste in music. Nevertheless, this was not important to Cher or to Camilletti when they were together.

Media pursuit of the couple was relentless. Cher and Rob were hounded wherever they went. She did not feel safe even in her own home, stating that reporters climbed over her fence, one incessantly rang her doorbell, and one man kicked in her front door.

Camilletti had a hard time dealing with the publicity. Because of the 18-year age difference between Cher and him, he was characterized as an opportunist and a "seedy hustler." Rob had acting ambitions, but his relationship with Cher was not helping him further his career. No one thought he was serious about acting.

The final blow came when the media reported that

Cher is accompanied to a party by her son, Elijah Blue, who often acts as his mother's escort. As a teenager Elijah went through a rebellious period, but eventually settled down as a musician with his own band.

the couple was going to marry. Reporters dubbed them Mr. and Mrs. Cher III. The rumor wasn't true, but that didn't keep photographers and reporters from swarming around Cher's home. Whenever she and Camilletti went out, photographers chased them, following their car in an attempt to get photos.

Cher has declared that her romance with Rob Camilletti was her most fulfilling relationship. But the publicity and pressure of being "Mr. Cher" was too much for him to handle, and the couple split up.

One day when Cher needed to go to a doctor's appointment, she devised a plan. She hid in a car driven by a friend while Rob drove out in another car. When he returned, an unfortunate incident occurred. To avoid hitting the photographers who had jumped into the driveway, Camilletti swerved and crashed the car.

In a bizarre turn of events, the photographers accused Rob of trying to kill them, and he was arrested. In spite of his and Cher's protests, he was briefly jailed until Cher paid his bail. Camilletti's sentence was a heavy fine and many hours of community service.

For Camilletti, the incident was the final indignity. His acting career was going nowhere, and he was being constantly harassed by the media, not to mention the humiliation he experienced in jail. Although Rob told Cher that he still loved her, she noted in her autobiography, he couldn't take this kind of life any longer, and he left.

When asked years later who had been the greatest love of her life, Cher didn't hesitate. "My relationship with Rob was the best," she declared. "He was so much fun. I felt that I was in really good hands when I was with him." Cher and Camilletti remain good friends and see each other from time to time.

In the early 1990s, Cher's acting career seemed to be at a standstill. She recorded a couple of albums but received no film offers. Still, she did not give up or lose her confidence. As she herself has said, "I make mistakes, I turn around and I come back."

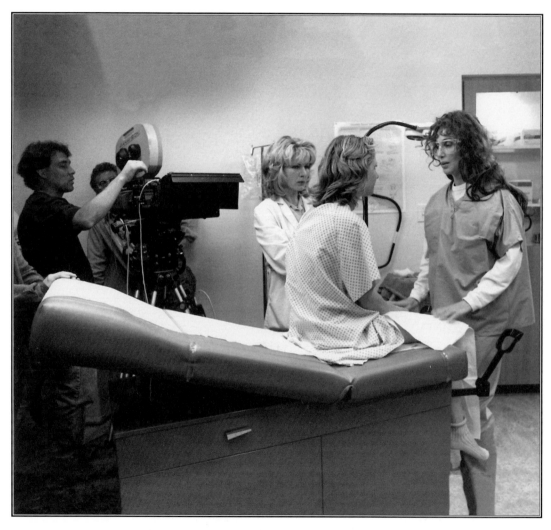

In the mid-1990s, an undaunted Cher took on a new challenge, directing an episode of the HBO film If These Walls Could Talk. *In one of the film's scenes, which she also directed, she plays a doctor (at right) in an abortion clinic.*

7

MAKING A COMEBACK

For about four or five years, Cher told *Rolling Stone,* life was "pretty quiet." No new movie roles, no new albums, no concert tours. "I just puttered around," she said. "I was kinda happy not to be Cher for a while."

Then, in 1995, a totally new career opportunity opened up. Cher learned that an exciting new television project was in the works. Actress Demi Moore was executive-producing a special movie for Home Box Office (HBO) called *If These Walls Could Talk.* The film would consist of three segments, each with a theme on abortion, and each story occurring in a different decade.

The first episode is set in the 1950s, when abortion was still illegal. Episode two takes place in the 1970s, after abortion had become legal. The third episode is set in the 1990s, and its story reflects some of the thinking and controversy surrounding abortion today.

The aim of *If These Walls Could Talk* was to show how people viewed abortion throughout U.S. history and the impact of abortion on women's lives. The film neither supports nor opposes abortion, but merely presents the plight of women caught up in difficult situations.

Cher agreed to act in one episode of *If These Walls Could Talk*, but only if she could also direct a segment. She starred in and directed the final segment.

In the first episode, a nurse played by Demi Moore undergoes an illegal abortion and is injured during what is obviously an unsafe procedure. The second segment focuses on Barbara, a married woman with three children, and it illustrates the difficult decision a woman with an unwanted pregnancy must face. Barbara, played by Sissy Spacek, is looking forward to resuming her career. Even though she is legally permitted to have the abortion, she is torn between her career and having the baby. In the end, she chooses to have the baby.

The last segment illustrates controversial issues surrounding abortion in the 1990s. A young pregnant woman, played by Anne Heche, arrives at an abortion clinic to find it under siege by a crowd of anti-abortion activists. Eventually the young woman makes it into the clinic, but the doctor, played by Cher, is murdered by an anti-abortion fanatic.

Aired on HBO in 1996, *If These Walls Could Talk* received praise from critics and audiences. It also achieved one of the highest ratings for an HBO movie. Cher was especially pleased with her experience making the film. "I must say I was very happy directing," she told *Ladies Home Journal*. "What's fun about being me right now is I have lots of opportunities if I just open myself up to them."

Cher also had the opportunity that year to return to music. She released *It's a Man's World*, her first album in more than five years. In general, the album received positive reviews, with some music reviewers commenting that Cher's voice sounded better than ever.

It's a Man's World presents a mix of music styles as well as some experimental material. For instance, the title song, a soul music number first made popular by

James Brown, was a departure for Cher's usual pop sound. Cher also sings an appealing bluesy version of "The Sun Ain't Gonna Shine Anymore."

Making the album wasn't easy for Cher. She later confided that she had suffered from terrible stage fright while recording. In the years since her last album, *Heart of Stone*—which had featured her hit "If I Could Turn Back Time"—she had barely sung at all, not even around the house or in the shower. However, Cher has learned to how to cope with her nervousness. As she confessed to *Rolling Stone,* "I've never gone in [the studio] feeling confident in my life. That's just the way I am. I just start doing it and hope I'll forget I'm feeling apprehensive."

Cher also has a tendency to play down her singing talent. Despite the obvious appeal of her husky voice, she claims that it is the *way* she sings that has more to do with her success than her natural ability. "I'm not the best singer in the world," she has explained. "I can't listen to my own voice. You see all your mistakes when you hear your own voice. . . . All the imperfections."

After having released the new album and starred in her directorial debut, Cher decided to return to major motion pictures. She signed on to a film called *Faithful,* originally a stage play. In it she plays the wife of a businessman who hires a hit man to murder her. Much of the movie focuses on Cher's character, who is tied to a chair most of the time. Ironically, she holds a long philosophical conversation with the hired executioner.

As this black comedy progresses, the victim and would-be killer develop a relationship as they converse about love, sex, and other weighty topics. The script is sometimes humorous such as the scene where the hit man phones his psychiatrist.

Released in 1996, *Faithful* did not translate well from the original stage play to the screen. Most of the action takes place in an upstairs bedroom, which gives

In the film Faithful, *Cher is menaced by Chas Palminteri, a killer hired by her husband. In this comeback big-screen effort, Cher was appealing, but the film was not a critical success.*

the film a claustrophobic mood. There is also not enough suspense. Audiences can easily figure out that the hit man is too good-natured to be a real threat.

Renowned movie critic Roger Ebert found *Faithful* mildly amusing, mostly because of the talent and appeal of Cher and her costars Ryan O'Neal and Chas Palminteri. Cher was an entertaining victim, and as usual she looked terrific. Despite Cher's appeal in her comeback film, *Faithful* was not a smash hit.

A more significant cinematic achievement for Cher was her next film, *Tea with Mussolini*. Directed and cowritten by Franco Zeffirelli, well known for his direction of movies such as Mel Gibson's *Hamlet* as well as operas, the film is partly based on Zeffirelli's life as a child. It tells the story of a young orphaned Italian boy under the guardianship of a group of eccentric Englishwomen. The time and place is 1930s Florence, Italy, during the fascist dictatorship of Benito Mussolini. Snobbish and living in their own fantasy world, the women think that Mussolini likes the English. As World War II approaches, the women seem oblivious to their danger and believe that if they could just have "tea with Mussolini," he would realize they were not a threat and would protect them.

In the film, Cher plays a very rich, flamboyant American socialite named Elsa, who visits Florence from time to time to buy art. Her presence among the Englishwomen is not always welcome. She is larger than life, melodramatic, and intensely materialistic. Her furs, jewels, and outsize hats jar with the plain fashion of the other women. As the film progresses, however, it becomes clear that Elsa is more complex than she seems. She is generous, kind, and vulnerable. Cher described her role as that of "a tart with a heart."

Cher has said that Zeffirelli had cast her from the beginning as the only one possible for the role of Elsa. "That's very seductive," she admitted, "when a director, especially a man, says that." Cher also claimed in an interview that she wished for and got the other members of the cast. According to Cher, the original actresses who were to play the English-women did not work out. Then Cher was asked with whom she would like to work, and she named Judi Dench, Maggie Smith, and Joan Plowright. She didn't name the other star, Lily Tomlin, who played an American archeologist.

Although Cher said she was a bit intimidated at first by working with such a formidable cast, she gave one of her finest film performances. Released in 1998, *Tea with Mussolini* showcased Cher's acting skills and reminded moviegoers of her power on the big screen. Critics also liked Cher's performance. One reviewer wrote in *Film Comment,* "It is only after she appears that you realize how sorely she's been missed from movie screens! For Cher is a star. That is, she manages the movie star trick of being at once a character and at the same time never allowing you to forget: that's Cher." *Entertainment Weekly* also admired her talent: "Always likable, always soft-focus, always strange, Cher does her darndest acting."

All the actors received praise for their performances in *Tea with Mussolini,* but the film itself was not as well received. Criticism centered on director Zeffirelli. While *Tea with Mussolini* was entertaining, reviewer Roger Ebert criticized it as a series of events or anecdotes rather than a story with a plot. *Entertainment Weekly* noted that the director placed too much emphasis on one-liners rather than on developing meaningful conversation among the characters. The same reviewer also criticized the film for a lack of "clarity or depth."

In the same year that *Tea with Mussolini* was released, Cher greatly impressed the public and her fans in an appearance in which she did not act or sing. She delivered a deeply moving eulogy at the funeral of former husband Sonny Bono.

In early January 1998, Sonny was killed in a skiing accident near Lake Tahoe in California. At the time, he was a U. S. congressman from California and was married to his fourth wife, Mary.

Cher was in London when she was awakened by a phone call from Chastity with the news of Sonny's death. Cher's reaction was immediate and stunned Chastity, who said she had never seen her mother behave in such a way. She became hysterical. "I just started sobbing and collapsed to my knees," Cher would later remember.

In the film Tea with Mussolini, *Cher shone as the flamboyant, rich American in Italy. She received critical accolades for her performance and reaffirmed her star status.*

Cher immediately arranged to take a flight to California. At London's Heathrow airport, the ever-present photographers captured a visibly shaken woman as she hastened to her plane. Once back in California, Cher stayed at a guest house at Sonny's Palm Springs home. Chastity and Elijah were with her to give comfort and support.

When a friend asked Cher to speak at Sonny's

funeral, she hesitated at first. The friend insisted, telling her that Sonny's family wanted her to do it. When Cher finally accepted, she spent two days writing the words she wanted to say. She wrote several drafts of her eulogy because, as she said, "I didn't want to blow it. I felt I had to repair all the damage and misconceptions about Sonny." She was determined that people would remember Sonny as the creator of their performances and how he loved to make people laugh.

Sonny had once told Cher that it was best not to look at a loved one in an open casket. A person's last memory of the deceased, he believed, should be of when they were alive. At the private wake before the funeral, Cher promised herself that she would not look at her former husband in his casket. She changed her mind, however, when Chastity went up to her father. As Cher stood with her daughter before the open casket, she glanced at Sonny's hands as they lay folded on his chest. She had always loved his hands, believing they were elegant and artistic. She wrote later that looking at Sonny's hands "made it all real for me."

Cher admitted that speaking about Sonny was the toughest performance she ever had to give. She confessed to being "terrified" and trying to control her emotions by gritting her teeth and locking her knees to keep her legs from buckling.

Despite her anxiety, at the January 9 funeral service in Palm Springs, Cher shared with the audience heart-felt remembrances of Sonny through the years. Poignant at times, her words made the listeners cry. At other moments, her humor broke through as she commented, "I know he's somewhere, loving this."

At the end, Cher spoke of how Sonny had always reminded her of a section in *Reader's Digest*, which she liked to read when she was young. It was "The Most Unforgettable Character I Ever Met." For Cher that character was Sonny.

A tearful Cher delivers a moving eulogy at the funeral of Sonny Bono, held in January 1998. She was determined to let people know what Sonny meant to her and how he had influenced her life.

At the cemetery after the service, Cher's last gesture to Sonny was to place her hand on his coffin and say to herself, "This is not good-bye."

Today, Cher claims that although they traded barbs with each other over the years, she and Sonny shared a great love. They may not have spoken for months at a time, but an unshakable bond connected them. As she said in an interview with *Ladies Home Journal* a year before his death, "Even if we don't say nice things about each other, it doesn't mean anything. I know Sonny too well."

Cher firmly believes that although Sonny is not

here in his earthly form, he is still here for her in spirit. In 1999 she even contacted a well-known psychic named James Van Praagh, who assured her that Sonny, in death, wanted her to know that he still loved her very much. That knowledge made Cher feel more connected to Sonny than ever. "I don't feel separated from him," she said.

In a recent interview, Cher revealed that she believed Sonny was still taking care of her. She believes that following his death, things began coming together for her. "I wouldn't be surprised if he's up there taking care of me," she remarked in an interview. "He did a good job of looking after me in the sixties and I'm quite happy for him to do it again."

In an affectionate tribute to Sonny, Cher hosted a television special on May 20, 1999, on CBS, called *Sonny and Me: Cher Remembers.* The program included clips from their old shows and home movies, and even enlarged family photos.

Cher confessed that as she was compiling the show, she had many emotional moments. As she looked through the mementos of their years together, she often felt tears coming on. In an interview given before taping the program, Cher reminisced about these memories. When she found his old fur vest from the 60s, for example, she remembered so many of the details from the day they decided to use it in their act. "It's so long ago," she said, "it's like another solar system."

Before Sonny's death, Cher had been in the middle of another project that also evoked many memories from years past. She had been compiling a collection of autobiographical essays of "first-time" events in her life. Appropriately called *The First Time*, the essay collection included incidents ranging from the light, such as the first film she saw, to the momentous, such as the Oscar she won.

Written with humor and honesty, Cher's essays

are about the events that helped shape her life and her career. She had almost finished the manuscript when Sonny died, and she was undecided about whether to include his death in the book. She feared that some reviewers would criticize her for capitalizing on the tragic event. But in the end Cher decided to be true to herself and reveal her feelings about Sonny's death. The last essay in the book is called *My First Tragedy*.

As Cher told *Rolling Stone*, "I couldn't ignore it, could I? I might have if I cared more about what people think than what I know is right for me. . . . I don't have to explain myself. I'd like for people to understand, but if they don't, well, that's the way things go."

The First Time, published in 1998, received glowingly positive reviews. Critics praised the book as a fun read and noted that it presented Cher as very real and likable. Even the prestigious and often negative *New York Times* gave the book a thumbs-up review, saying that *The First Time* revealed Cher to be a "funny, gutsy" woman who is "down to earth" and "genuine."

In the book Cher elaborates on her childhood poverty, how she finally met her birth father, and her awareness of being a "dark" child. She reveals her feelings about Sonny and the other men in her life, and candidly describes her relationship with her children. Several of the "firsts" describe exciting or devastating moments in her singing and acting career. *The First Time* is a lively mix of all the small and large events that make up the personality of Cher.

In 1999 Cher added to her achievements with the release of a new song, "Strong Enough," which made the top 40 hit list. In a cooperative venture, she sang with superstars Whitney Houston, Tina Turner, and Brandy on a new CD, *VHI Divas Live '99*. And Cher's CD *Believe* went platinum four times. Her public

Cher added author *to her list of accomplishments with the publication of her memoirs, entitled* The First Time. *In November 1998 she appeared at a book store to sign her new book and her CD album* Believe.

appearances included singing "The Star-Spangled Banner" at the 1999 Super Bowl and opening the yearly sale at London's most exclusive department store, Harrod's.

As the 1990s came to a close, Cher could look back on an array of impressive achievements. As the new year approached, she was considering a number of projects to take on in the 21st century.

Audiences never know quite what to expect when Cher makes an appearance. Still beautiful and flamboyant, she appears onstage at the 2000 Primetime Emmy Awards in a long blonde wig to announce the winner for Lead Actor in a Miniseries or Movie.

FIFTY-SOMETHING AND FABULOUS

On September 12, 2000, Cher attended the Emmy Awards ceremony in Los Angeles. She had been nominated for an Emmy for her performance in the 1999 special *Cher: Live in Concert from the MGM Grand in Las Vegas*. Dressed in a sparkling red sequined blazer and studded designer jeans, her long dark hair gleaming and lustrous, the star dazzled the crowd.

Although Cher did not receive an Emmy that night, which instead went to comedian Eddie Izzard, her appearance was truly memorable. In the second half of the ceremony, Cher presented the award for Best Performance by an Actress in a Comedy Series to Patricia Heaton of *Everyone Loves Raymond*. But when she appeared onstage, she looked completely different. She had changed into a white silk jacket and sported long, almost platinum blond hair. "I was so upset about not winning that my hair turned blond," she quipped to the audience before presenting the award.

Cher can always be counted on to do the unexpected, which is just what she did with her latest music project. In November 2000, Cher released an album called *Not Commercial*. The official title is *Not.Com.mercial* because it can only be downloaded from the Internet. She has stressed that it is not a follow-up to *Believe*, which was dance oriented. *Not.Com.mercial* is deeply personal and features the first songs she has ever written by herself.

The songs in the album reveal Cher's intense feelings about her personal experiences. In "Sisters of Mercy," Cher sings of the time she spent in a Catholic orphanage. Her pain is raw and real as she labels the nuns "mothers of shame" and "twisters of truth." Cher reveals her distress over the suicide of rock singer Kurt Cobain in "The Fall." She recounts her shame in thoughtlessly ignoring and stepping over a homeless woman when she sings "Our Lady of San Francisco." As a tribute to Sonny, Cher includes an antiwar song that he wrote, "Classified 1-A."

Cher expected to get some negative criticism for "Sisters of Mercy," but she claims the song is not a condemnation of the Catholic Church. "I have known many wonderful and loving nuns in my life," she says. She does admit, however, that "[The album] is very un-Cher like. But if people really knew me, it is very Cher. But it's so dark, I have to put a sticker on it. I don't want kids buying it. I write like I speak—not exactly like a sailor, but colorful."

Cher decided to release the CD on the Internet because she believes that the Internet allows her the freedom to experiment with more personal choices. She also wanted to make the album available to people who might not want to buy a conventional CD.

According to Cher, she has no great hopes or expectations for the success of *Not.Com.mercial*. She made the album for herself and wants to share it with others regardless of whether or not reviewers like it. She professes that if people don't like it, that's fine with her.

Cher does reassure fans of her usual pop sound that she is also working on a more commercial, more

STAR Club CHER   FICHE N° **1392**

« ALL OR NOTHING »

All or nothing...

I've been standing out in the rain
I've been calling your name
I've got that lonely feeling again
Calling out your name

Do you hear me ?
Do you want me ?

Refrain
Baby it's all or nothing now
Don't wanna run and I can't walk out
You're breaking my heart
If you leave me now
Don't wanna wait forever
Who do you think you're fooling ?
Who do you think you're fooling ?
Baby it's all or nothing
Baby it's all or nothing now (now, now, now)

I've been trying to get to your heart
But I'm chasing shadows
We keep falling further apart
So near and you're so far

Do you care now ?
Do you know how ?

Refrain

Sometimes when you touch me
I just can't help myself
Can't help myself
Desire makes me weak
Desire makes me weak

Do you care now ?
Do you know how ?

Baby it's all or nothing
I don't wanna run and I can't walk out
You're breaking my heart
If you leave me
Don't wanna wait forever
Baby it's all or nothing now
Don't wanna run and I can't walk out
You're breaking my heart
If you leave me now
Don't wanna wait forever
Who do you think you're fooling ?
Who do you think you're fooling ?
Baby it's all or nothing
Baby it's all or nothing now
Now...

Trois ans après l'album It's A Man's World, notre star préférée fait son grand retour avec Believe. Ce nouvel album est résolument orienté vers la dance. Encore une fois, notre belle Américaine (et Arménienne, ne l'oublions pas) a su s'entourer de talents pour la seconder. Cher a dédié son album à la mémoire de Sonny Bono, son ex-mari, mort accidentellement en skiant. Elle estime qu'elle ne serait pas ce qu'elle est aujourd'hui s'il n'avait pas été là. Cette mort lui a permis de se rendre compte à quel point Sonny et elle étaient liées pour la vie... Sur ce troisième single extrait de l'album, la superstar exige des explications de son partenaire amoureux. Elle souhaite que tout soit clair entre eux : soit il cesse de la tromper et elle lui sera fidèle, soit il va voir ailleurs et c'en sera fini de leur couple... Ce sera « tout ou rien » (c'est la traduction du titre).

dance-oriented CD as a follow-up to *Believe*. It will be available in stores sometime in 2001.

The versatile performer shows no signs of slowing down. The year 2000 was especially rewarding for her. In the first two months of the year, she was nominated for an American Music Award for Favorite Adult Contemporary Artist and won her first Grammy for "Believe," which was awarded the year's Best Dance Recording. She had also been nominated for two other Grammy Awards in the Record of the Year category and Best Pop Album category.

Spring and summer of 2000 found Cher receiving a Blockbuster Entertainment Award for Favorite Female Pop Artist. In August she sang at the Democratic convention in Los Angeles, serenading departing President Bill Clinton with "If I Could Turn Back

Cher launched the new millennium when she moved into the cyber world. Fans can now see her familiar face and read the lyrics to her songs by logging onto the Internet.

Cher continues to perform at a variety of events, including political rallies. Here, former vice president Al Gore and wife, Tipper Gore, thank Cher for her efforts at a Democrat fund-raising effort held two months before the 2000 election.

Time." Brutally honest as always, she told Clinton that she hadn't voted for him, but she did think he had been a good president.

The next month, she introduced Vice President Al Gore to the audience at a huge fund-raising gala in Camden, New Jersey. Dressed in peekaboo black lace, Cher emerged onto the stage to thunderous applause. Her greeting nearly matched that of the vice president himself.

Engaged with all these activities, Cher has decided that she no longer minds being in her 50s, as she did in 1996, when she turned the half-century mark. "I feel like I have a lot on my horizon," she says. "At first I didn't like the idea of being in my 50s at all. . . . But you have to always be figuring out new ways to stay in the game, you know?"

One project that Cher hopes will keep her in the game is playing the role of Mrs. Robinson in a musical version of *The Graduate,* which is bound for Broadway in 2001. Based on the 1967 film, *The Graduate* tells the story of a young college graduate who is seduced by the glamorous, older, and married Mrs. Robinson, the neighbor next door. This famed seductress was originally played by Anne Bancroft, who was nominated for an Academy Award for Best Supporting Actress.

The musical version debuted in London in spring 2000 and featured film actress Kathleen Turner as Mrs. Robinson. She was succeeded in the role by Jerry Hall, model and former wife of Mick Jagger. Since Cher hasn't appeared on Broadway in almost 20 years, the role of Mrs. Robinson will be a welcome challenge. She is also looking forward to returning to New York City, where her acting career began.

For three years, Cher has also been working on the television project, *Fashion Emergency,* which she executive produces for cable TV. In that capacity, she supervises the entire production from conception to finished taped product, and is responsible for obtaining the financing. *Fashion Emergency* is based on a British show called *Style Challenge,* for which Cher purchased the rights. The show features two guests who receive style makeovers in beauty and wardrobe. Cher's flair for beauty and dress is invaluable to the show.

Obviously Cher enjoys extending her creative energies in many different directions. With the success of her directorial debut in *If These Walls Could Talk,* she has been looking for other behind-the-scenes work to become involved in. Cher is not afraid to risk failure or try new things. As she once told *Interview,* "I get really bored with one thing so I enjoy being creative in different ways. If I get interested in something, I no longer think of it as work. I think of it as play. And I just get really excited about it, like learning something new, like when I was little. If I can do it, then let me do it. And if I'm terrible at it, everyone will tell me. Because that's what life is about, changing what you were before."

Despite having a rather hectic professional life, Cher confesses to being more mellow than she used to be and to slowing down her personal life. She is not as concerned with being a fashion plate, as she once was. She even removed her tattoos with laser treatments because the markings simply no longer appealed to her.

More often than not, Cher spends weekends at her home in Malibu, California, overlooking the ocean. She has turned her house into a cozy nest where she can unwind by burning scented candles and listening to meditation music.

Cher's favorite companions these days are Chastity and Elijah Blue. Chas visits several times a week, and mother and daughter enjoy cooking together and playing board games. They also speak openly with each other. Chastity talks to Cher about her partners and has revealed to her mother that she believes some of the men her mother dates are not suitable.

Cher offers her own advice and tells her daughter she should settle down and have a baby. "She'd love to be a grandmother," Chastity has revealed. "She loves playing with her assistant's nephew and going off to the toy store for friends' kids. But she's never pressured me."

As far as her own romantic life is concerned, Cher has been single for a long time now. She has not been seriously involved with anyone since she broke up with Bon Jovi guitarist Richie Sambora in 1993. She is comfortable being alone, and likes the independence she has gained.

There is another reason for staying single—it's not that easy, she has said, to meet men who really attract her. Another part of the problem is Cher's superstar status. "It's easy for women to hang out with men who are famous," she says, "but no man wants to be Mr. Cher." Still, she does confess that she looks forward to the day when she will meet someone with whom she can share her life again.

Cher is adamant that in spite of her desire to meet somebody special, she won't search among the typical Hollywood crowd. "I'm not at all involved in the Hollywood community, which a lot of people say is a big mistake. I can't be bothered. I never felt it was worth it," she told *Interview* magazine.

Looking back, Cher has few regrets—with a couple of exceptions: she wishes that she had turned down the notorious infomercials, and she also feels it was a mistake to be so honest about her cosmetic surgery. Although she admits to having her nose and teeth fixed, she insists that the media was incorrect in its claims that she had her ribs removed and implants placed in her cheeks.

What is most worthwhile, in Cher's view, is continuing to entertain and grow as an artist. Ever since she was a little girl, Cher has felt she had something special. Even as she grows older, she still feels compelled to explore that specialness and develop new ways to express it to her public. Cher remains as youthful and full of life as ever.

As she told *People,* "You have to figure out new, creative ways to stay vital, interested, have new dreams. Maybe I'll come back as a cowboy. Maybe next time I'll do better."

If her reincarnation brings anything close to the glamour and excitement she has given her audience of the past 40 years, it will be spectacular and memorable—like the woman herself.

CHRONOLOGY

1946   Cherilyn Sarkisian born to Jackie Jean Crouch and John Sarkisian on May 20 in El Centro, California

1950s   Moves several times in California; attends many different elementary schools

1961   Enrolled by stepfather in Montclair Prep high school; suffers from the learning disability dyslexia

1962   Drops out of high school; moves to Los Angeles; meets Sonny Bono

1964   Sings backup vocals for rock and roll recordings; records first hit single on music charts, "Baby Don't Go"; exchanges unofficial marriage vows with Sonny

1965   Records with Sonny first hit single "I Got You Babe"

1966   Records first solo single, "Bang, Bang (My Baby Shot Me Down)"

1967   Produces with Sonny the film *Good Times*, which receives disasterous reviews

1969   Marries Sonny; films *Chastity* with Sonny; gives birth to daughter, Chastity

1971   *The Sonny and Cher Comedy Hour* debuts on CBS; solo single "Gypsies, Tramps and Thieves" is certified gold and hits number one spot; releases album *Cher*

1973   Single "Half-Breed" becomes gold record; meets record company executive David Geffen

1974   Files for divorce from Sonny; gold-selling single "Dark Lady" is released

1975   Debuts *Cher*, solo television show; receives final divorce decree from Sonny; marries Gregg Allman

1976   Releases album *I'd Rather Believe in You*; son Elijah Blue Allman born; reunites briefly with Sonny on a new TV show, *The Sonny and Cher Show*

1977   Divorces Gregg Allman

1979   Releases disco album *Take Me Home*; album and single "Take Me Home" are certified gold

1982   Appears on Broadway in *Come Back to the Five and Dime, Jimmy Dean, Jimmy Dean*; receives Golden Globe nomination for her performance in film version of the play

1983   Appears in *Silkwood*; wins Golden Globe Award for her role

1984   Stars in *Mask*; nominated for Best Supporting Actress Oscar
for *Silkwood*

1985   Wins Best Actress Award at Cannes Film Festival for starring role
in *Mask*

1986   Begins relationship with Robert Camilletti

1987   Appears in three major films: *Witches of Eastwick, Suspect,* and
Moonstruck; releases chart-topping hits "I Found Someone"
and "We All Sleep Alone"

1988   Wins Best Actress Oscar for *Moonstruck*; releases album *Heart of
Stone,* which sells more than three million copies in the United
States; launches perfume line Uninhibited

1989   *Heart of Stone* and "If I Could Turn Back Time" are certified gold;
makes live concert tour

1990   Stars in film *Mermaids*

1992   Releases gold-selling album *Love Hurts* and singles "Love and
Understanding" and "Save Up All Your Tears"

1995   Releases album *It's a Man's World* with hit single "One by One"

1996   Returns to films with *Faithful;* stars in and directs segment of HBO
special *If These Walls Could Talk*

1998   Delivers eulogy at funeral of Sonny Bono, who died in skiing accident
on January 5; films *Tea with Mussolini*; releases *Believe* with single
of same title; publishes autobiographical memoir, *The First Time*

1999   Hosts television tribute to Sonny Bono; sings the National Anthem
at the Super Bowl; single "Believe" sells more than 1.7 million
copies in Britain and is number one on the *Billboard* Hot 100
Singles list; album *Believe* goes quadruple platinum; named by
Advocate magazine as one of the "25 Coolest Women"

2000   Wins Grammy for Best Dance Recording for "Believe"; nominated
for Grammy Awards for Record of the Year and Best Pop Album;
nominated for an Emmy for Best Performance in a Live Action
Show; awarded Favorite Female Pop Artist by Blockbuster
Entertainment Awards

DISCOGRAPHY

Albums

1965   *All I Really Want to Do*
        Look at Us

1966   *Sonny Side of Cher*
        Alfie (film sound track)

1967   *Good Times* (film sound track)
        With Love

1968   *Cher's Golden Greats*
        Backstage

1970   *3614 Jackson Highway*

1971   *Cher*

1972   *Mama Was a Rock and Roll Singer*
        Bittersweet White Light
        Cher's Greatest Hits
        Cher Sings the Hits
        Hits of Cher
        Foxy Lady

1974   *Very Best*
        Greatest Hits
        Dark Lady

1976   *Stars*
        I'd Rather Believe in You

1977   *Two the Hard Way*
        Cherished

1978   *This Is Cher*

1979   *Take Me Home*
        Prisoner

1980   *Black Rose*

1981   *The Best of Cher, Vol. 1*
        The Best of Cher, Vol. 2

1982   *I Paralyze*

1985   *Golden Greats*

1987   *Cher*

1988   *Heart of Stone*

1989   *Outrageous*

1990   *Down: The Best of Cher*

1991   *Best of Cher*
         Love Hurts

1996   *It's a Man's World*

1998   *Believe*
         Black Rose

1999   *Bittersweet: The Love Songs Collection*
         If I Could Turn Back Time
         Bang Bang: The Early Years

2000   *Not Commercial*

Hit Singles

1964   "Baby Don't Go"

1965   "I Got You, Babe"

1966   "Bang, Bang (My Baby Shot Me Down)"

1967   "The Beat Goes On"

1971   "Gypsies, Tramps & Thieves"

1973   "Half-Breed"

1977   "You're Not Right for Me"

1999   "Strong Enough"

FILMOGRAPHY

1967 *Good Times*

1969 *Chastity*

1982 *Come Back to the Five and Dime, Jimmy Dean, Jimmy Dean*

1983 *Silkwood*

1985 *Mask*

1987 *The Witches of Eastwick*
      Suspect
      Moonstruck

1990 *Mermaids*

1996 *If These Walls Could Talk* (HBO; also codirected)
      Faithful

1999 *Tea with Mussolini*

Books and Periodicals:

Cher. *The First Time*. New York: Random House, 1999.

Dunn, Jancee. "Cher." *Rolling Stone,* 19 September 1996.

Gerosa, Melina. "I'm Cher." *Ladies Home Journal,* November 1996.

Jerome, Jim. "Being Cher." *People,* 25 May 1998.

King, Tom. *The Operator: David Geffen Builds, Buys and Sells the New Hollywood*. New York: Random House, 2000.

Klein, Roberta, "Conjuring a Surprise Sanctuary in Miami Beach." *Architectural Digest,* October 1996.

Naylor, David. "Cher Shares." *Ladies Home Journal,* July 1999.

Quirk, Lawrence J. *Totally Uninhibited: The Life and Wild Times of Cher*. New York: William Morrow and Company, 1991.

Roberts, Bruce. "More Cher." *Interview,* October 1994.

Russell, Lisa. "Cher." *People,* 15–22 March 1999.

Siegel, Micki. "She Won't Stop." *TV Radio Mirror,* March 1974.

Tusher, Will. "How Can You Marry This Man?" *TV Radio Mirror,* November 1975.

Udovitch, Mim. "Q & A: Cher." *Rolling Stone,* 15 April 1999.

Weitzman, Elizabeth. "Straight Up Cher." *Interview,* December 1998.

Wickens, Barbara. "The Cher Effect." *Maclean's,* 6 March 1989.

Websites:

Internet Movie Data Base. *http://www.imdb.com*

Women.Com Interview. "Cher: Staying Power," by Sheryl Altman. *http://www.women.com/entertainment/interviews/cher/cher.html*

INDEX

INDEX

PICTURE CREDITS

page

2: OLUSA

12: Eric Gaillard/Reuters/ NMI

15: Zoran Bozicevic/ Newsmakers

16: Everett Collection

19: New Millennium Images

20: Everett Collection

23: New Millennium Images

24: New Millennium Images

26: Everett Collection

29: New Millennium Images

32: Motion Pictures Int'l/ NMI

33: Reuters Photo Archives

34: CBS/NMI

37: AP/Wide World Photos

38: Everett Collection

43: AP/Wide World Photos

45: Hulton Getty/Keystone Collection/NMI

46: New Millennium Images

48: New Millennium Images

51: Everett Collection

53: Everett Collection

56: Everett Collection

58: AP/Wide World Photos

61: New Millennium Images

62: Everett Collection

64: Reed Saxon/AP/Wide World Photos

66: AP/Wide World Photos

69: New Woman/NMI

70: Everett Collection

74: Richard Ellis/AFP/ NMI

77: Tammie Arroyo/ OLUSA

78: OLUSA

80: Everett Collection

84: Everett Collection

87: Everett Collection

89: Nick Ut/Reuters/NMI

92: Rose Prouser/Reuters/ NMI

94: Lucy Nicholson/AFP/ NMI

97: New Millennium Images

98: William Thomas Cain/ Newsmakers

Cover Photo: Gregg Deguire/London Features Int'l, Ltd.

Connie Berman is a writer and editor who has worked on more than 20 books about such celebrities as Tom Cruise, Mel Gibson, Diana Ross, Debra Winger, Don Johnson, Linda Ronstadt, and Caroline Kennedy. She once worked with Dolly Parton on a scrapbook about Parton's life. Connie was the coproducer of *The Yuppie Handbook: A Guide for Young Urban Professionals* (Simon and Schuster). She lives outside Philadelphia, Pennsylvania. This is her first book for Chelsea House.

Matina S. Horner was president of Radcliffe College and associate professor of psychology and social relations at Harvard University. She is best known for her studies of women's motivation, achievement, and personality development. Dr. Horner has served on several national boards and advisory councils, including those of the National Science Foundation, Time Inc., and the Women's Research and Education Institute. She earned her B.A. from Bryn Mawr College and her Ph.D. from the University of Michigan, and holds honorary degrees from many colleges and universities, including Mount Holyoke, Smith, Tufts, and the University of Pennsylvania.